A CHANGE OF SEASONS

Folk-Art Quilts and Cozy Home Accessories

Bonnie Sullivan

A Change of Seasons:
Folk-Art Quilts and Cozy Home Accessories
© 2016 by Bonnie Sullivan

Martingale®
19021 120th Ave. NE, Ste. 102
Bothell, WA 98011-9511 USA
ShopMartingale.com

Printed in China
21 20 19 18 17 16   8 7 6 5 4 3 2 1

**Library of Congress Cataloging-in-Publication Data
is available upon request.**

ISBN: 978-1-60468-746-0

MISSION STATEMENT

We empower makers who use fabric and yarn
to make life more enjoyable.

CREDITS

PUBLISHER AND
CHIEF VISIONARY OFFICER
Jennifer Erbe Keltner

CONTENT DIRECTOR
Karen Costello Soltys

MANAGING EDITOR
Tina Cook

ACQUISITIONS EDITOR
Karen M. Burns

TECHNICAL EDITOR
Nancy Mahoney

COPY EDITOR
Sheila Chapman Ryan

PRODUCTION MANAGER
Regina Girard

COVER AND
INTERIOR DESIGNER
Adrienne Smitke

PHOTOGRAPHER
Brent Kane

ILLUSTRATOR
Christine Erikson

SPECIAL THANKS

*Thanks to Joe and Sharon Pruskowski of
Woodinville, Washington, for allowing the
photography for this book to take place in their home.*

Contents

INTRODUCTION • 5

Spring

Spring Blossoms • 6

Spring Fling • 12

Spring Has Sprung • 24

Spring Chick • 30

Autumn

Harvest Home • 58

Autumn Star • 64

Dance of the Autumn Leaves • 70

Autumn Crow • 74

Summer

Sweet Summer • 34

Summer Celebration • 40

Watermelon Banner • 50

Sunflowers • 54

Winter

Winter Wonders • 78

Holly in My Heart • 84

The Stockings Were Hung • 92

Frosty • 104

BONNIE'S TECHNIQUES • 107

RESOURCES • 111

ABOUT BONNIE • 112

Introduction

When I was a child, I couldn't wait for winter. I loved watching big snowflakes fall from a gray winter sky—something that was a bit of an unusual treat in Oregon's Willamette Valley. I was so excited to sled down the hill by the school on an old cookie sheet. I have memories of putting plastic bread wrappers over my socks before I slid my feet into my shoes to go out in the snow and play, and coming home to a nice hot cup of homemade cocoa. The anticipation of the Christmas season with its colorful lights and delicious aromas—as well as time spent making homemade ornaments, caroling, and the gathering of family—filled my heart with such warmth.

As I grew older, things changed. I found myself longing impatiently for the next season. In winter, I couldn't wait for spring to come with its promise of leaves on the trees and longer days. When spring finally arrived, I became anxious for summer, for school vacation, and for days that never seemed to end. And then there was the excitement of fall right around the corner and returning to school to see friends and pick out a Halloween costume for trick-or-treating.

I still love the gathering of family and friends during the Christmas season and my heart skips a beat with the first snowflakes of the year. But I've come to appreciate all the seasons and try to breathe in every aspect of what makes each season special while it's here. Spring with its new budding leaves on the trees and the earth coming alive with blossoms of so many colors and shapes. And oh, those warm, long days of summer. In autumn the trees on my street explode with color and I love seeing the first *V* formation of geese flying south. I would be hard-pressed now to choose a season as my favorite. Each season has such extraordinarily unique gifts to offer and I adore them all!

I hope you enjoy the projects in this book that reflect some of the things that make each season special to me.

Bonnie

Spring Blossoms

designed and made by BONNIE SULLIVAN

Hand-dyed wool in light spring colors illustrates this season of new beginnings.
A rustic frame echoes the color of the background linen, tying the whole piece together.

FINISHED SIZE: 23" x 19", framed

LINEN

20" x 24" rectangle of linen for background (see "Background Fabric" at right for details)

WOOL

All wool sizes are for felted wool.

5" x 12" rectangle of brown for vase and pussy willow stems

6" x 12" rectangle of green for stems and leaves

4" x 11" rectangle of white for bunny and bleeding heart centers

2" x 6" rectangle of blue tweed for bird

1½" x 3½" rectangle of blue for bird's wing

2½" x 3" rectangle of light-blue plaid for bunny's bow and vase center

3" x 5" rectangle of pink for bleeding hearts

4" x 5" rectangle of tan tweed for pussy willows

3" x 4" rectangle of yellow for daffodil petals

1½" x 2" rectangle of light gold for daffodil cup

1½" x 1¾" rectangle of dark gold for daffodil center and bird's beak

OTHER MATERIALS

½ yard of 18"-wide lightweight, paper-backed fusible web

Thread to match wool colors

19" x 23" frame, with a 16" x 20" interior opening

16" x 20" piece of foam-core board

PEARL COTTON

Colors listed below are for Valdani pearl cotton.
See "Resources" on page 111.

Tea-Dyed Stone (light gray) for bunny's legs

Withered Green for veins on leaves and bleeding heart stems

Black for bird's eye and bunny's eye

Background Fabric

Don't be afraid to try something new! I found the coarsely woven linen I wanted in the drapery department of a fabric store. I washed the fabric to soften it up a bit. A piece of old ticking with a subtle stripe would also work great, like the one I used in the Dance of the Autumn Leaves banner on page 70.

PREPARING THE APPLIQUÉS

Refer to "Working with Wool" on page 107 for detailed information.

1. From the green wool, cut two ⅜" x 12" strips for the bleeding heart stems and one ⅜" x 5" strip for the daffodil stem. Cut all strips on the straight of grain.

2. Cut the brown wool into two ⅜" x 12" strips for the pussy willow stems.

3. Using the patterns on pages 10 and 11, trace each appliqué shape the number of times indicated on the pattern onto the paper side of the fusible web. Cut out each shape about ⅛" outside the drawn lines. See "Trace to Fit" on page 107 for a time-saving tip.

4. Following the manufacturer's instructions, fuse each shape, glue side down, onto the wrong side of the designated wool color. Cut out each shape exactly on the drawn lines.

APPLIQUÉING THE DESIGN

See "Decorative Stitches" on page 110 as needed.

1. To mark a 16" x 20" rectangle on the linen rectangle, lay the piece of cardboard or glass that came with the frame in the center of the rectangle. Using a pencil, carefully trace all around the cardboard or glass. The marked rectangle is your design boundary; be sure to keep your design within the lines.

2. Using the photo on page 8 as a guide and starting with the vase, bunny, and bird, arrange the appliqué pieces on the background. Pin the stems in place, curving them as shown. Note that you'll need to tuck some pieces under another piece, such as the bottom of the rabbit under the vase. Fuse the appliqué pieces to the background.

3. Using thread that matches the wool appliqués, whipstitch the pieces in place.

4. Use the stone pearl cotton and an outline stitch for the definition lines for the bunny's legs.

5. Use the green pearl cotton and an outline stitch to embroider the bleeding hearts to the stems. In the same way, stitch the center vein on one leaf.

6. Use a single strand of black pearl cotton to make a French knot for the bird's eye. Use a double strand of black pearl cotton to make a larger French knot for the bunny's eye.

FINISHING

Place the foam-core board on the wrong side of the embroidered piece, centering the stitched design. Fold the edges of the fabric over the foam-core board, making sure the fabric is taut but not distorted. Tape the fabric in place. Insert the backing into the frame and secure it with the clips that came with the frame.

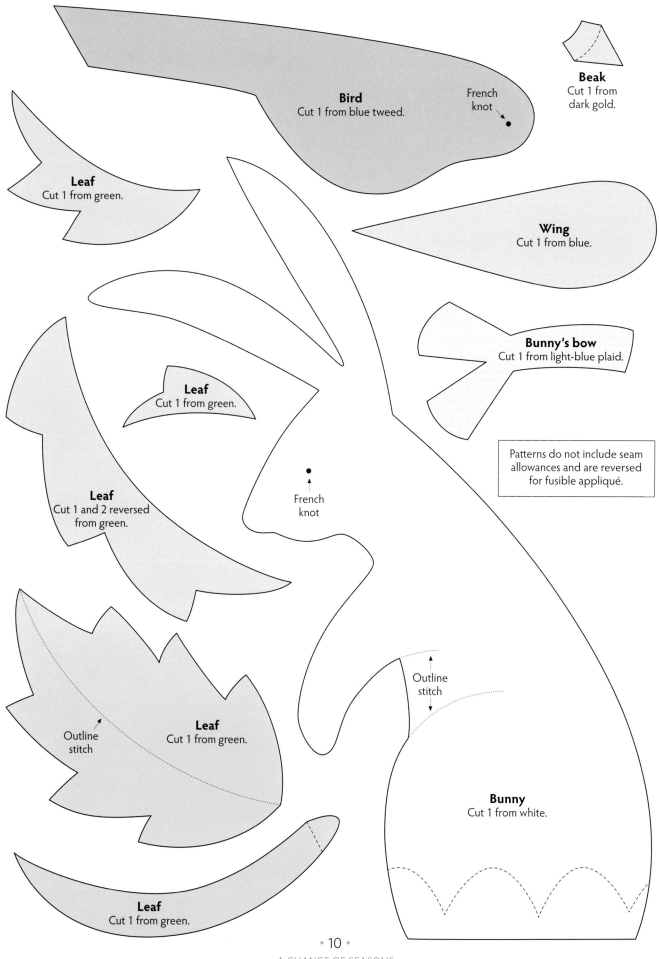

Bird
Cut 1 from blue tweed.

French knot

Beak
Cut 1 from dark gold.

Leaf
Cut 1 from green.

Wing
Cut 1 from blue.

Bunny's bow
Cut 1 from light-blue plaid.

Leaf
Cut 1 from green.

Patterns do not include seam allowances and are reversed for fusible appliqué.

Leaf
Cut 1 and 2 reversed from green.

French knot

Outline stitch

Outline stitch

Leaf
Cut 1 from green.

Outline stitch

Bunny
Cut 1 from white.

Leaf
Cut 1 from green.

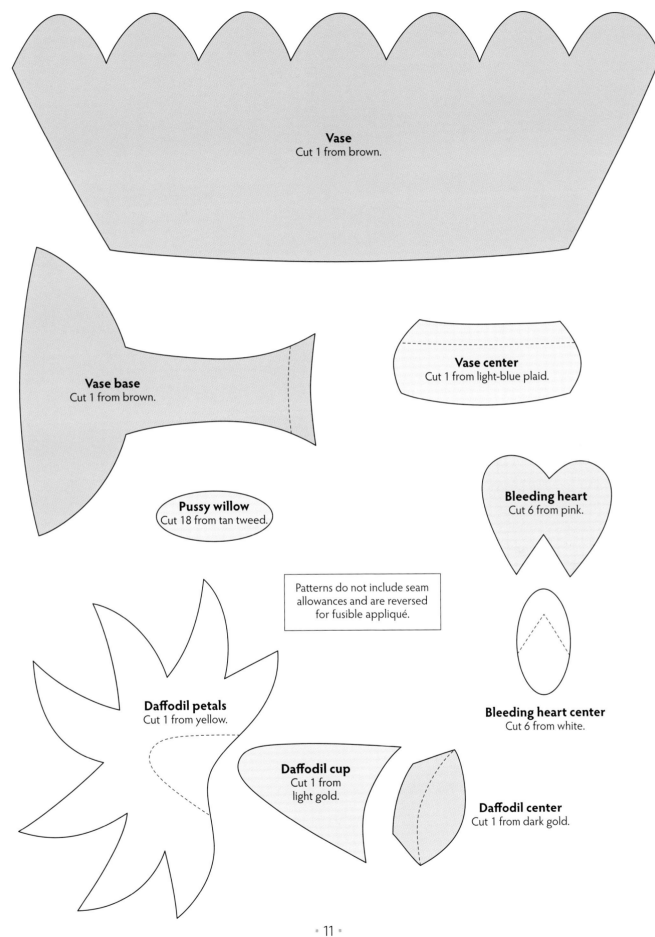

Vase
Cut 1 from brown.

Vase base
Cut 1 from brown.

Vase center
Cut 1 from light-blue plaid.

Bleeding heart
Cut 6 from pink.

Pussy willow
Cut 18 from tan tweed.

Patterns do not include seam allowances and are reversed for fusible appliqué.

Bleeding heart center
Cut 6 from white.

Daffodil petals
Cut 1 from yellow.

Daffodil cup
Cut 1 from light gold.

Daffodil center
Cut 1 from dark gold.

Spring Fling

designed by BONNIE SULLIVAN, pieced by MARJORIE McCANSE,
appliquéd by MARJORIE McCANSE and BONNIE SULLIVAN, and quilted by PAM PARVIN

Birds' nests and flowers are heralds of spring. Combine them with green-and-cream patchwork in a quilt that's bright and cheerful.

FINISHED SIZE: 57" x 57"
FINISHED BLOCK: 16" x 16"

FLANNEL

Yardage is based on 42"-wide flannel fabric.

2⅝ yards of cream herringbone for blocks and
    setting triangles
⅝ yard *each* of 3 green plaids for blocks (label as A,
    B, and C)
⅝ yard *each* of 2 cream-and-tan plaids for blocks
    (label as E and F)
1⅛ yards of green tweed for blocks and binding (label
    as D)
1 fat quarter (18" x 21") of cream print for blocks

WOOL

All wool sizes are for felted wool.

1 fat quarter (16" x 24") of green for stems and leaves
3" x 4" rectangle of yellow-green for base
    of daffodil buds
11" x 11" square of brown plaid for nests
8" x 8" square of light blue for eggs
8" x 12" rectangle of purple for daisies
5" x 6" rectangle of pink for bleeding hearts
3" x 4" rectangle of white for bleeding heart centers
7" x 8" rectangle of yellow for daffodil petals
    and buds
3" x 4" rectangle of light gold for daffodil cups
2" x 3" rectangle of dark gold for daffodil centers
3½" x 5" rectangle *each* of 3 blues for hyacinths

OTHER MATERIALS

3¾ yards of fabric for backing
63" x 63" piece of batting
1⅛ yards of 18"-wide lightweight, paper-backed
    fusible web
Thread to match wool colors

CUTTING

From the cream herringbone, cut:
4 rectangles, 18" x 21"
1 strip, 8½" x 42"; crosscut into 4 squares, 8½" x 8½"
11 strips, 2½" x 42"; crosscut into:
    32 rectangles, 2½" x 8½"
    32 rectangles, 2½" x 4½"
2 squares, 12¾" x 12¾"; cut the squares into quarters
    diagonally to yield 8 triangles
2 squares, 6¾" x 6¾"; cut the squares in half
    diagonally to yield 4 triangles

From *each* of the 3 green plaids (A, B, and C), cut:
1 rectangle, 18" x 21" (3 total)
5 squares, 5" x 5" (15 total)
24 squares, 2½" x 2½" (72 total)

Continued on page 15

Continued from page 12

From the green tweed (D), cut:
7 strips, 2½" x 42"
1 rectangle, 18" x 21"
5 squares, 5" x 5"
24 squares, 2½" x 2½"

From *each* of the 2 cream-and-tan plaids (E and F), cut:
4 squares, 8½" x 8½" (8 total)
10 squares, 5" x 5" (20 total)

From the cream print, cut:
4 squares, 8½" x 8½"

MAKING THE APPLIQUÉD BLOCKS

Refer to "Working with Wool" on page 107 for detailed information.

1. Lay out one cream herringbone, one cream-print, and two different cream-and-tan 8½" squares in a four-patch arrangement as shown. Join the squares into rows. Press the seam allowances open. Join the rows and press the seam allowances open. Make four blocks.

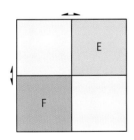

Make 4.

2. From the green wool, cut 16 strips, ⅜" x 11", for the flower stems in all the blocks.

3. Using the patterns on pages 22 and 23, trace each appliqué shape the number of times indicated on the pattern onto the paper side of the fusible web. Cut out about ⅛" outside the drawn lines. See "Trace to Fit" on page 107.

4. Following the manufacturer's instructions, fuse each shape, glue side down, onto the wrong side of the designated wool color. Cut out each shape exactly on the drawn lines.

5. Using the photos on page 14 as a guide and starting with the nest, arrange the appliqué pieces on each Four Patch block. Pin the stems in place, curving them as shown. Note that you'll need to tuck some pieces under another piece, such as the ends of the stems under the nest. Fuse the appliqué pieces to the background.

6. Using thread that matches the wool appliqués, whipstitch the pieces in place.

MAKING THE PINWHEEL BLOCKS

1. Draw a diagonal line from corner to corner on the wrong side of each cream-and-tan 5" square. Layer a marked E square right sides together with a green C 5" square. Sew ¼" from each side of the marked line. Cut the squares apart on the drawn line. Press the seam allowances open to reduce bulk. Trim the half-square-triangle units to measure 4½" x 4½". Repeat to make 10 units from each fabric combination as shown (40 total).

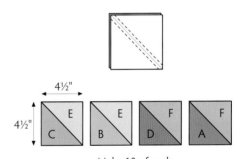

Make 10 of each.

2. Lay out four different half-square-triangle units from step 1 as shown to make a pinwheel unit. Join the units into rows, and then join the rows. Press all seam allowances open. Make nine units, measuring 8½" x 8½". You'll have one extra unit of each fabric combination.

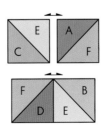
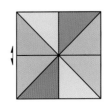

Make 9.

Keep Organized

At a glance, this quilt may look scrappy, but upon closer inspection, you'll see that each fabric is placed very specifically. These instructions are for making a quilt that looks exactly like the one shown. To stay on track, label each of your green and cream fabrics before you start, and then keep like units together by color name until they're needed. You may find zip-top plastic bags or small binder clips are helpful in keeping like fabrics together.

If you prefer a more carefree assembly, mix and match the greens and creams as desired to make the number of each unit called for. 🕊

3. Layer cream herringbone and green 18" x 21" rectangles, right sides together. Beginning at the corner of the rectangles, place a long ruler at a 45° angle to the bottom edge of the rectangles. Cut along the edge of the ruler. Using the first cut as a guide, cut 2¼"-wide bias strips across the rectangles.

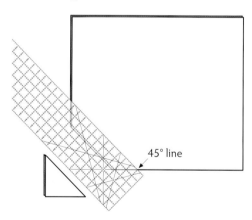

45° line

4. With the strips still right sides together, sew a scant ¼" from the raw edge on *both* long sides of the strips, making sure not to pull or stretch the bias edges. Cut the strips into half-square-triangle units, measuring 2½" from the stitched line (not the raw edge point) as shown. Cut 36 half-square-triangle units. Press the seam allowances open. The units should measure

2½" x 2½". Repeat the process, using the remaining cream herringbone and green 18" x 21" rectangles. You should have 144 half-square-triangle units total.

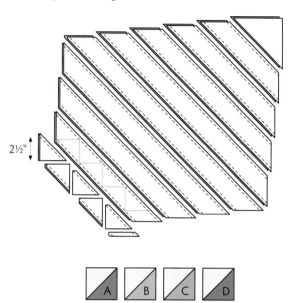

2½"

Make 36 of each.

5. Lay out four different half-square-triangle units from step 4 to make a corner unit. Join the units into rows, and then join the rows. Press all seam allowances open. Make six of each fabric combination as shown (24 total). Set aside the remaining half-square-triangle units for now.

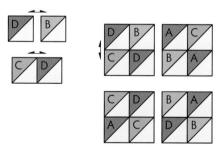

Make 6 of each.

6. Draw a diagonal line from corner to corner on the wrong side of each green 2½" square. Place a marked B square on one end of a cream herringbone 2½" x 4½" rectangle, right sides together and raw edges aligned. Stitch along the marked line. Trim away the excess fabrics, leaving a ¼" seam allowance. Press the seam

allowances open to reduce bulk. Place a marked D square on the other end of the rectangle. Sew, trim, and press to make a flying-geese unit. Make four flying-geese units of each fabric combination as shown.

Make 4 of each.

7. Repeat step 6, sewing a marked green square on one end of a cream herringbone 2½" x 4½" rectangle. Make two of each unit as shown.

Make 2 of each.

8. Repeat step 6, sewing marked green squares on both ends of a cream herringbone 2½" x 8½" rectangle. Make four of each unit as shown.

Make 4 of each.

9. In the same way, sew a marked green square on one end of a cream herringbone 2½" x 8½" rectangle. Make two of each unit as shown.

Make 2 of each.

10. Lay out two different half-square-triangle units from step 4, one flying-geese unit from step 6, and one unit from step 8 to make a side unit. Join the units and press the seam allowances open. Make four of each fabric combination as shown (16 total).

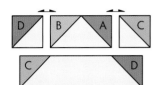

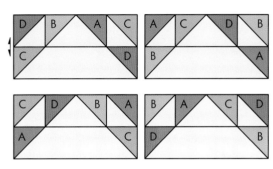

Make 4 of each.

11. Lay out one of each corner unit from step 5, one of each side unit from step 10, and one pinwheel unit from step 2 as shown. Join the units into rows, and then join the rows. Press all seam allowances open. Make one block.

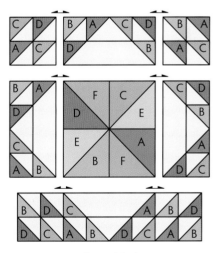

Center block.
Make 1.

12. Lay out three corner units from step 5, two side units from step 10, one unit and one reversed unit from step 7, one unit and one reversed unit from step 9, two half-square-triangle units from step 4, and one pinwheel unit from step 2. Join the units into rows, and then join the rows. Press all seam allowances open. Make one of each side block as shown.

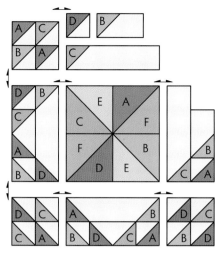

Side block.
Make 1 of each shown below.

Top.
Unit A.

Bottom.
Unit B.

Left side.
Unit C.

Right side.
Unit D.

13. Lay out two corner units from step 5, one side unit from step 10, one unit and one reversed unit from step 7, one unit and one reversed unit from step 9, two half-square-triangle units from step 4, and one pinwheel unit from step 2. Join the units into rows, and then join the rows. Press all seam allowances open. Make one of each corner block as shown.

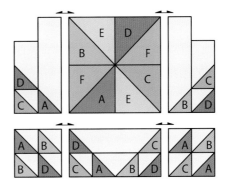

Corner block.
Make 1 of each as shown below.

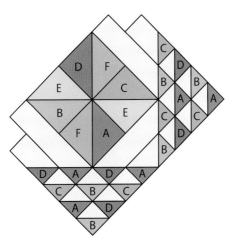

Top-left corner.
Unit E.

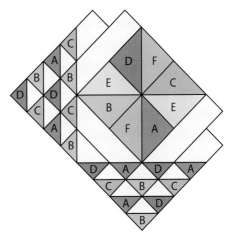

Top-right corner.
Unit F.

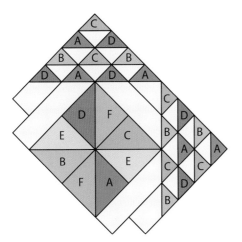

Bottom-left corner.
Unit G.

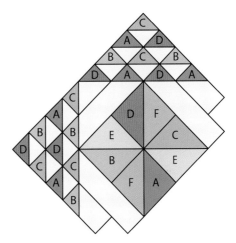

Bottom-right corner.
Unit H.

Planned Scrappy

Each green and cream fabric in the Pinwheel blocks is placed in the same spot for each block. The impression is of a scrappy quilt, yet the color placement is precisely orchestrated. This strategy applies to the appliquéd blocks also, where the tan squares alternate from the sides to the top and bottom of the blocks.

ASSEMBLING THE QUILT TOP

1. Lay out the blocks and cream herringbone 6¾"
   and 12¾" triangles in diagonal rows as shown in
   the quilt assembly diagram below.

2. Join the blocks and side triangles into rows.
   Press the seam allowances open.

3. Join the rows; press the seam allowances open.
   Add the corner triangles last. Press the seam
   allowances open.

4. Trim and square up the quilt top, making sure to
   leave ¼" beyond the last seam intersection for
   the seam allowances.

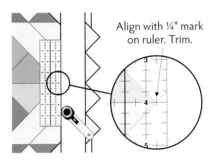

Align with ¼" mark
on ruler. Trim.

FINISHING

For more details on any of the following steps, go to
ShopMartingale.com/HowtoQuilt for free,
downloadable information.

1. Layer the quilt top with batting and backing;
   baste the layers together.

2. Machine quilt as desired. Trim the batting and
   backing so the edges are even with the quilt top.

3. Use the green tweed 2½"-wide strips to make
   and attach binding.

Quilt assembly

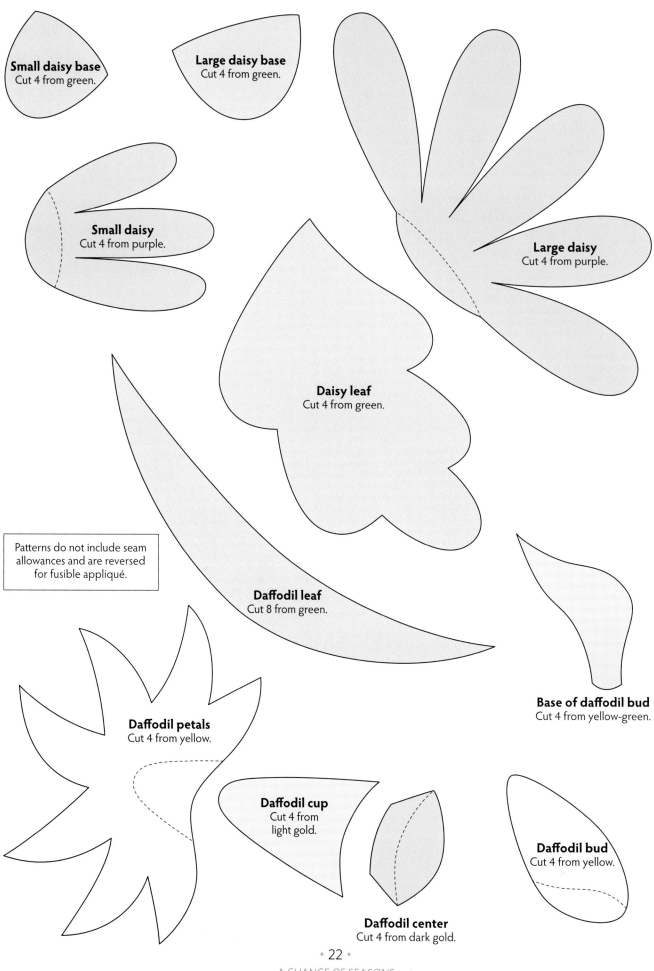

Small daisy base
Cut 4 from green.

Large daisy base
Cut 4 from green.

Small daisy
Cut 4 from purple.

Large daisy
Cut 4 from purple.

Daisy leaf
Cut 4 from green.

Patterns do not include seam allowances and are reversed for fusible appliqué.

Daffodil leaf
Cut 8 from green.

Base of daffodil bud
Cut 4 from yellow-green.

Daffodil petals
Cut 4 from yellow.

Daffodil cup
Cut 4 from light gold.

Daffodil center
Cut 4 from dark gold.

Daffodil bud
Cut 4 from yellow.

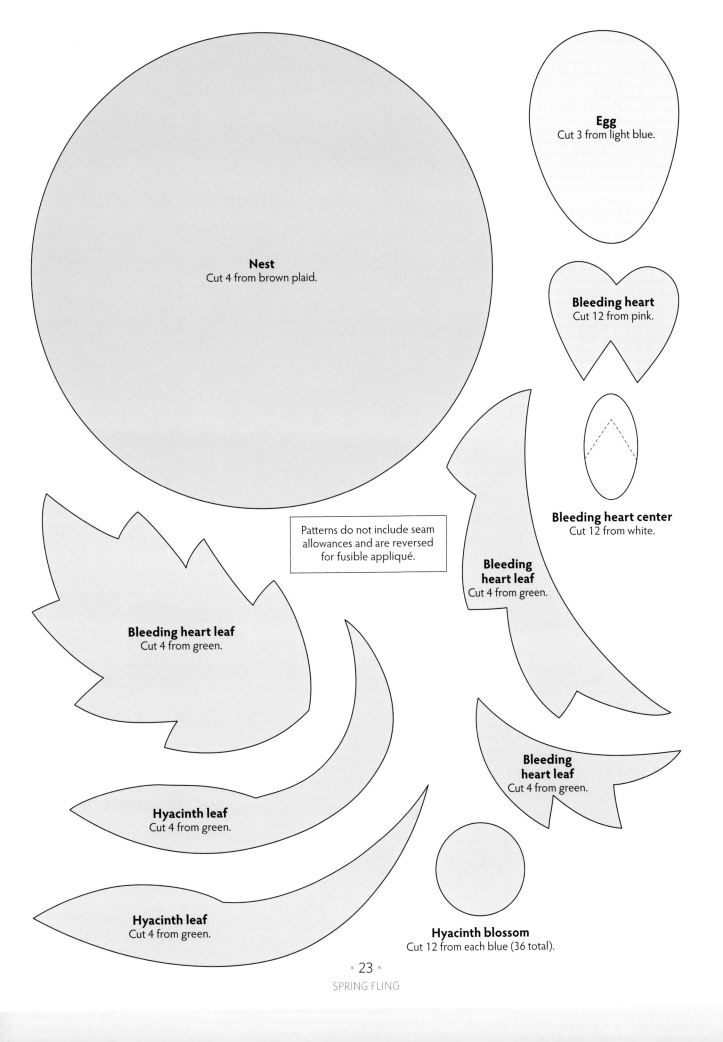

Egg
Cut 3 from light blue.

Nest
Cut 4 from brown plaid.

Bleeding heart
Cut 12 from pink.

Bleeding heart center
Cut 12 from white.

Patterns do not include seam allowances and are reversed for fusible appliqué.

Bleeding heart leaf
Cut 4 from green.

Bleeding heart leaf
Cut 4 from green.

Bleeding heart leaf
Cut 4 from green.

Hyacinth leaf
Cut 4 from green.

Hyacinth leaf
Cut 4 from green.

Hyacinth blossom
Cut 12 from each blue (36 total).

Spring Has Sprung

designed and made by BONNIE SULLIVAN

A throw pillow is a quick way to brighten up a room.
Welcome spring with a beribboned bunny and cheerful blooms.

FINISHED PILLOW: 26" x 14"

WOOL

All wool sizes are for felted wool.

2 pieces, *each* 15" x 27", of light gray for pillow front
  and back*
1 fat quarter (16" x 24") of blue-and-gray
  houndstooth for ruffle
8" x 18" rectangle of cream bouclé for rabbit
5" x 13" rectangle of green for bleeding heart stems
  and leaves
3" x 12" rectangle of dark green for daffodil stems
  and leaves
5" x 6" rectangle of blue for bow
4" x 6" rectangle of light-brown plaid for birds
3" x 4" rectangle of brown tweed for birds' wings
2" x 4" rectangle of dark gold for daffodil centers and
  birds' beaks
2" x 6" rectangle of gold for daffodil cups
6" x 8" rectangle of yellow for daffodil petals
2" x 10" rectangle of pink for bleeding hearts
3" x 4" rectangle of cream for bleeding-heart centers

OTHER MATERIALS

Thread to match wool colors
White thread for rabbit's eye
Heavy-duty thread for gathering ruffle
Black button, ½" diameter, for rabbit's eye
Polyester fiberfill for stuffing
Freezer paper

If the wool is at least 54" wide, you'll need ½ yard.

PEARL COTTON

Colors listed below are for Valdani pearl cotton.
See "Resources" on page 111.

Tarnished Gold for birds' legs and feet
Withered Green for bleeding heart stems and leaves
Black for birds' eyes

CUTTING

From the blue-and-gray houndstooth, cut:
8 strips, 1½" x 24"

PREPARING THE APPLIQUÉS

Refer to "Working with Wool" on page 107 for
detailed information.

1. From the green wool, cut two ⅜" x 13" strips for
   the bleeding heart stems.

2. From the dark-green wool, cut three ⅜" x 10"
   strips for the daffodil stems.

3. Using the patterns on pages 28 and 29 and the
   freezer-paper method described on page 108,
   trace each appliqué shape the number of times
   indicated on the pattern onto the unwaxed side
   of the freezer paper.

4. Press the shiny side of each shape onto the
   designated wool color. Cut out each shape
   exactly on the drawn lines.

ASSEMBLING THE PILLOW

See "Decorative Stitches" on page 110 as needed.

1. Using the photo above as a guide and starting with the rabbit, arrange the appliqué pieces on one of the light-gray pieces. Pin the appliqués in place, curving the stems as shown. Trim the stems to length as needed. Note that you'll need to tuck some pieces under another piece, such as the stems under the leaves.

2. Using thread that matches the wool appliqués, whipstitch them in place.

3. Use gold pearl cotton and two rows of outline stitching for the birds' legs. Use gold pearl cotton and one row of outline stitching for the birds' feet.

4. Use green pearl cotton and an outline stitch to embroider the bleeding heart blossoms to the stems. Using green pearl cotton, embroider a fly stitch in the center of each bleeding heart leaf.

5. Use a doubled strand of black pearl cotton to make French knots for the birds' eyes. Using white thread, sew a black button in place for the rabbit's eye.

6. Using a 120" length of heavy-duty thread, hand sew a row of gathering stitches ⅜" from one edge of a blue-and-gray strip. Continue sewing from one strip to the next until all of the strips are connected, gathering the ruffle pieces as you go.

Easy Does It!

Gathering a wool strip couldn't be easier. There's no need to cut a strip double the width and fold it in half, since wool won't fray like cotton will. Simply gather along one raw edge and you're done. Rustic and charming all in one. 🕊

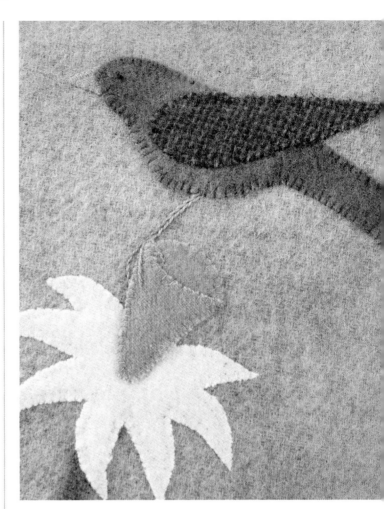

7. Adjust the amount of gathering so that the long length of ruffle goes all around the pillow. Pin the ruffle in place on the right side of the pillow front as shown. Using a ⅜" seam allowance, sew the ruffle in place.

⅜"

8. With right sides together, sew the pillow front and back together, making sure the ruffle is between the two layers. Stitch on top of the previously stitched line. Leave an 11" to 12" opening along the bottom edge for turning. Turn the pillow right side out. Stuff the pillow with polyester fiberfill. Close the opening with a slip stitch.

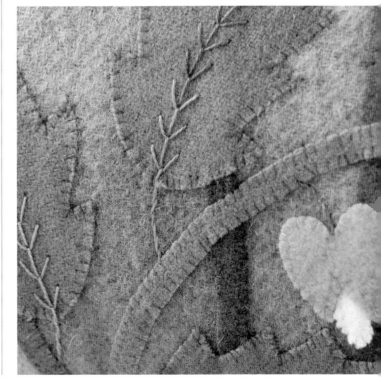

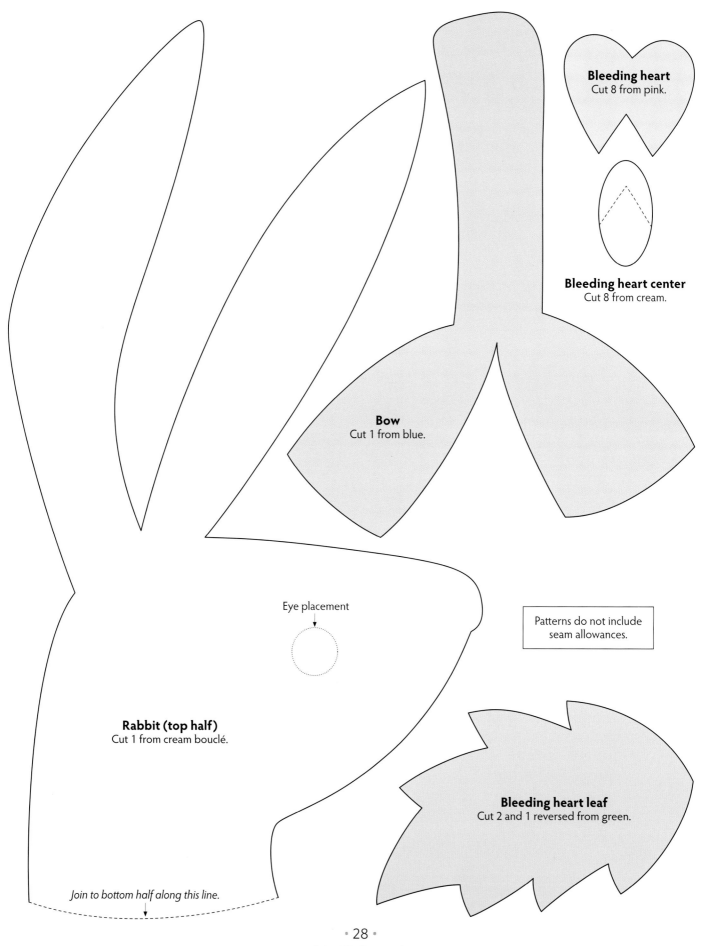

Bleeding heart
Cut 8 from pink.

Bleeding heart center
Cut 8 from cream.

Bow
Cut 1 from blue.

Eye placement

Patterns do not include
seam allowances.

Rabbit (top half)
Cut 1 from cream bouclé.

Bleeding heart leaf
Cut 2 and 1 reversed from green.

Join to bottom half along this line.

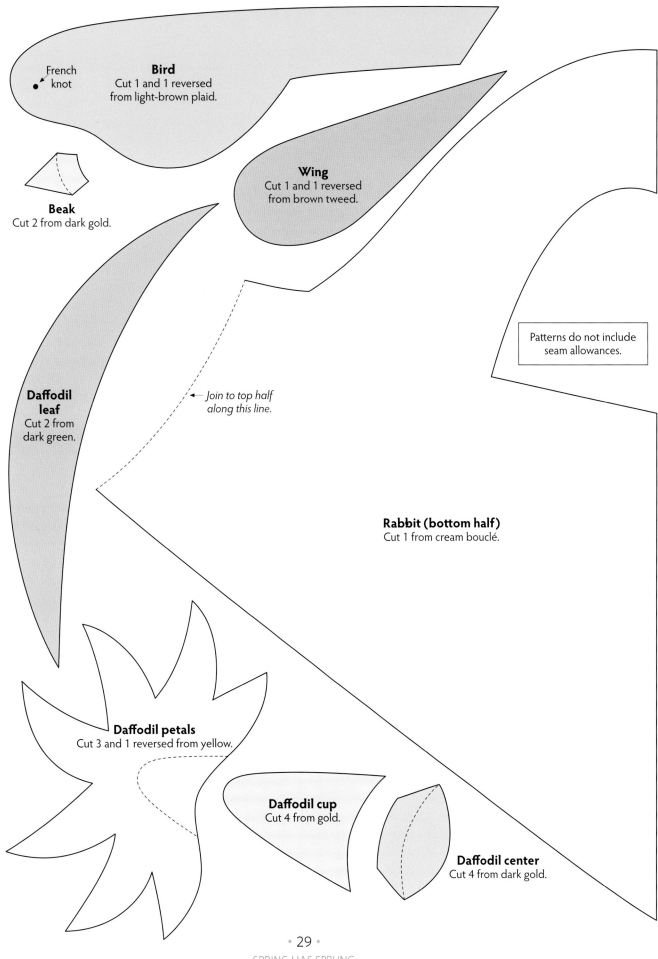

French knot

Bird
Cut 1 and 1 reversed from light-brown plaid.

Beak
Cut 2 from dark gold.

Wing
Cut 1 and 1 reversed from brown tweed.

Patterns do not include seam allowances.

Daffodil leaf
Cut 2 from dark green.

← *Join to top half along this line.*

Rabbit (bottom half)
Cut 1 from cream bouclé.

Daffodil petals
Cut 3 and 1 reversed from yellow.

Daffodil cup
Cut 4 from gold.

Daffodil center
Cut 4 from dark gold.

Spring Chick

designed and made by BONNIE SULLIVAN

Soft, sweet, and perched on a candlestick, this chick can be used as a pincushion or as a decoration to welcome the warmer months.

FINISHED CHICK BODY: 3½" tall x 6" long

WOOL

All wool sizes are for felted wool.

9" x 13" rectangle of yellow for chick's body and wing

3" x 3" square of light pink for large flower

2" x 2" square of dark pink for small flower

2" x 4" rectangle of green for leaves

1" x 1½" rectangle of gold for chick's beak

OTHER MATERIALS

2 black beads, ⅛" diameter, for chick's eyes

1 off-white decorative button, 1" diameter, for flower center

1 pink shank button, ½" diameter, for flower center

18" length of green floral wire for stem

Green floral tape for stem

Black heavy-duty thread

Wooden candlestick, 2½" tall

Heavy-duty wire and permanent glue (such as E-6000)

Polyester fiberfill for stuffing

Freezer paper

Drill

ASSEMBLING THE SPRING CHICK

Use a ¼" seam allowance throughout.

1. Using the patterns on page 33 and the freezer-paper method described on page 108, trace each appliqué shape the number of times indicated on the pattern onto the unwaxed side of the freezer paper.

2. Press the shiny side of each shape onto the right side of the designated wool color. Cut out each shape exactly on the drawn lines.

3. Layer the two chick bodies right sides together and pin in place. Slip the beak between the two pieces so that the tip of the beak is inside the body pieces and pin in place. Sew around the chick body, making sure to catch the beak in the seam and leaving a 2" opening at the bottom of the chick for turning. Trim the excess wool from the tail and head of the chick. Clip the curves. Turn the chick right side out through the opening. Stuff the chick with polyester fiberfill. Close the opening with a slip stitch.

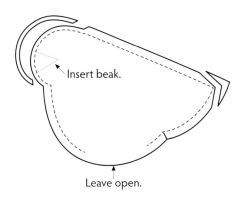

Insert beak.

Leave open.

4. With right sides together, sew all the way around one pair of wing pieces. Trim the excess wool from the pointed end of the wing and around the curved end. On the underside of the wing, make a slit in the center of the wing. Turn the wing right side out through the slit. Press and whipstitch the slit closed. (You don't have to be too neat, as the slit will not show.) Repeat to make a second wing.

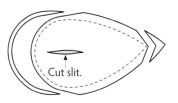

Cut slit.

5. Using black heavy-duty thread, sew a bead to each side of the chick's head, pulling on the thread to make a slight indentation where the eyes will be.

6. For the flower, thread the pink and off-white buttons on the floral wire, placing them in the center of the wire. Fold the wire in half so that both ends of the wire are even. Center the small dark-pink flower on top of the large light-pink flower and pierce the two flowers with the ends of the wire as shown. Gather the center of the green leaf. Insert the leaf between the two ends of the wire, directly below the pink flowers. Twist the wires under the leaf to hold it in place. Continue twisting the wires together until you reach the end of the wire. Trim the twisted wire stem to 6" long. Wrap floral tape around the wire stem for a finished look.

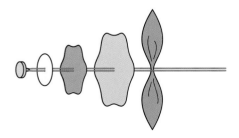

7. Position a wing on each side of the chick as shown in the photo on page 31. Pin the wings in place. Place the flower stem on one side of the chick, tucking it under the chick's wing. On each side, whipstitch the front half of each wing in place.

8. Using a drill bit that's about the same diameter as the heavy-duty wire, drill a tiny hole in the center of the candlestick. Insert a small, firm wire into the hole so that about 2" of the wire extends above the rim of the candlestick holder. Glue the wire in place. Insert the wire into the underbelly of the chick to hold it in place.

Wooden Candlestick

I used an old wooden candlestick for the base of the chick. I painted it a light green and rubbed a little antiquing glaze on it. If you're lucky, perhaps you can find an old painted candlestick with great patina.

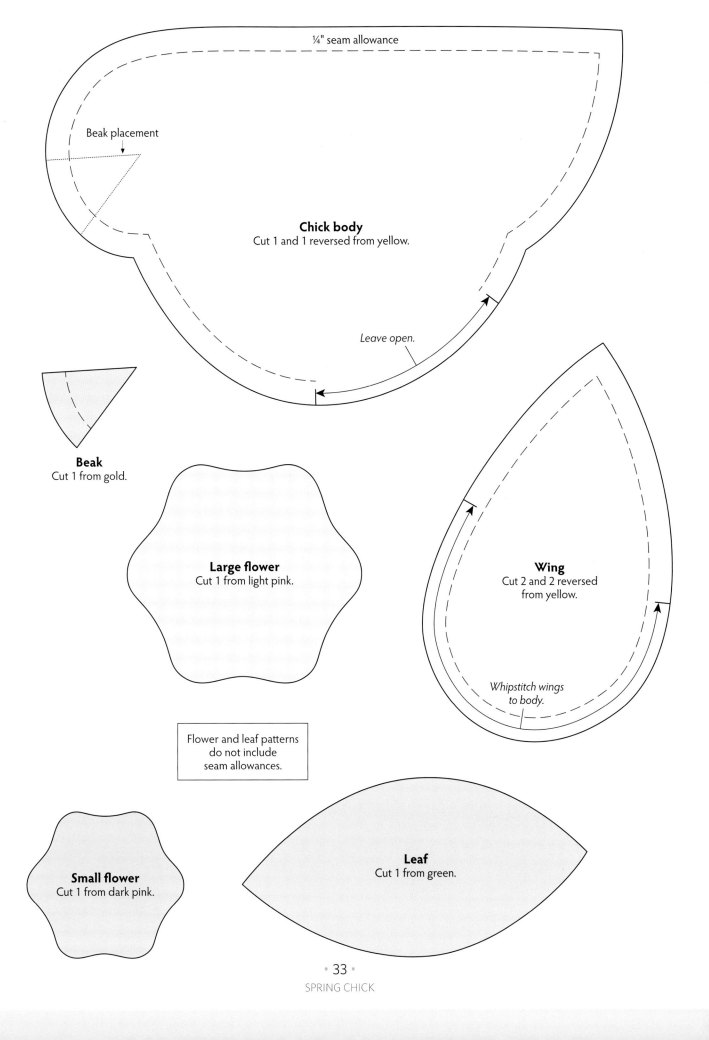

¼" seam allowance

Beak placement

Chick body
Cut 1 and 1 reversed from yellow.

Leave open.

Beak
Cut 1 from gold.

Large flower
Cut 1 from light pink.

Wing
Cut 2 and 2 reversed
from yellow.

*Whipstitch wings
to body.*

Flower and leaf patterns
do not include
seam allowances.

Small flower
Cut 1 from dark pink.

Leaf
Cut 1 from green.

Sweet Summer

designed and made by BONNIE SULLIVAN

Bees buzz around sunflowers, and the bluebird and cherries remind us of summer's bounty. A weathered black frame is the perfect finishing touch.

FINISHED SIZE: 23" x 19", framed

LINEN

20" x 24" rectangle of linen for background (see "Background Fabric" on page 6 for details)

WOOL

All wool sizes are for felted wool.

8" x 8" square of green for leaves and stems
6" x 9" rectangle of gold for sunflowers, petals, and bird's beak
6½" x 8" rectangle of gray herringbone for vase
2½" x 3" rectangle of dark gray for vase decorations
6" x 7½" rectangle of golden brown for bee skep
2½" x 2½" square of dark-brown check for bee-skep door
1½" x 2½" rectangle *each* of 3 reds for cherries
2" x 5" rectangle of black tweed for sunflower centers
4" x 6" rectangle of blue for bird
1½" x 4" rectangle of blue plaid for bird's wing
1" x 2" rectangle of yellow for bees

OTHER MATERIALS

½ yard of 18"-wide lightweight, paper-backed fusible web
Thread to match wool colors
Black 6-strand embroidery floss or black thread
Removable marking pen (such as a Frixion pen)
19" x 23" frame, with a 16" x 20" interior opening
16" x 20" piece of foam-core board

PEARL COTTON

Colors listed below are for Valdani pearl cotton. See "Resources" on page 111.

Olive Green for cherry branches
Tarnished Gold for cherry stems, bird's leg, and bird's foot
Aged Black (charcoal) for cherry leaves and bee skep
Black for bees and bird's eye

PREPARING THE APPLIQUÉS

Refer to "Working with Wool" on page 107 for detailed information.

1. Using the patterns on pages 38 and 39, trace each appliqué shape the number of times indicated on the pattern onto the paper side of the fusible web. Cut out each shape about ⅛" outside the drawn lines. See "Trace to Fit" on page 107 for a time-saving tip.

2. Following the manufacturer's instructions, fuse each shape, glue side down, onto the wrong side of the designated wool color. Cut out each shape exactly on the drawn lines.

Soften It Up

Linen makes a great background for wool appliqué, but new linen off the bolt can be quite stiff. I like to wash and dry it before using it to make it softer and easier to work with.

APPLIQUÉING THE DESIGN

1. To mark a 16" x 20" rectangle on the linen rectangle, lay the piece of cardboard or glass that came with the frame in the center of your background. Using a pencil, carefully trace all around the cardboard or glass. The marked rectangle is your design boundary; be sure to keep your design within the lines. (See "Use a Basting Line" on page 9 for an optional way to mark the design boundary.)

2. Using the photo above as a guide and starting with the bee skep, vase, and bird, arrange the appliqué pieces on the background. Pin the stems in place, curving them as shown. Note that you'll need to tuck some pieces under another piece, such as the bottom of the bee

skep under the vase. Use a removable marking pen to mark the cherry branches to make leaf placement easier. I use a Frixion pen to mark the branches. The lines from the Frixion pen will disappear when you iron the pieces in place. *Do not* use a water-soluble marker as the heat of the iron will permanently set the lines. Fuse the appliqué pieces to the background.

3. Using thread that matches the wool appliqués, whipstitch the pieces in place.

4. Use green pearl cotton and two rows of outline stitching for the cherry branches.

5. Use gold pearl cotton and an outline stitch for the stems of the cherries. Use gold pearl cotton to embroider two rows of outline stitching for the bird's leg and one row of outline stitching for the bird's foot.

6. Use black pearl cotton and a satin stitch for the stripes on the bees. Use straight stitches for the bees' stingers and antennae. Use a doubled strand of black pearl cotton to make a French knot for the bird's eye.

7. Using a running stitch and aged-black pearl cotton, stitch along the center of each cherry leaf. Use aged-black pearl cotton and a fly stitch to embroider the definition lines on the bee skep.

8. Use black thread or one strand of embroidery floss and an outline stitch to embroider the bees' wings.

FINISHING

Place the foam-core board on the wrong side of the embroidered piece, centering the stitched design. Fold the edges of the fabric over the foam-core board, making sure the fabric is taut but not distorted. Tape the fabric to the board and then insert the backing into the frame. Secure with the clips that came with the frame.

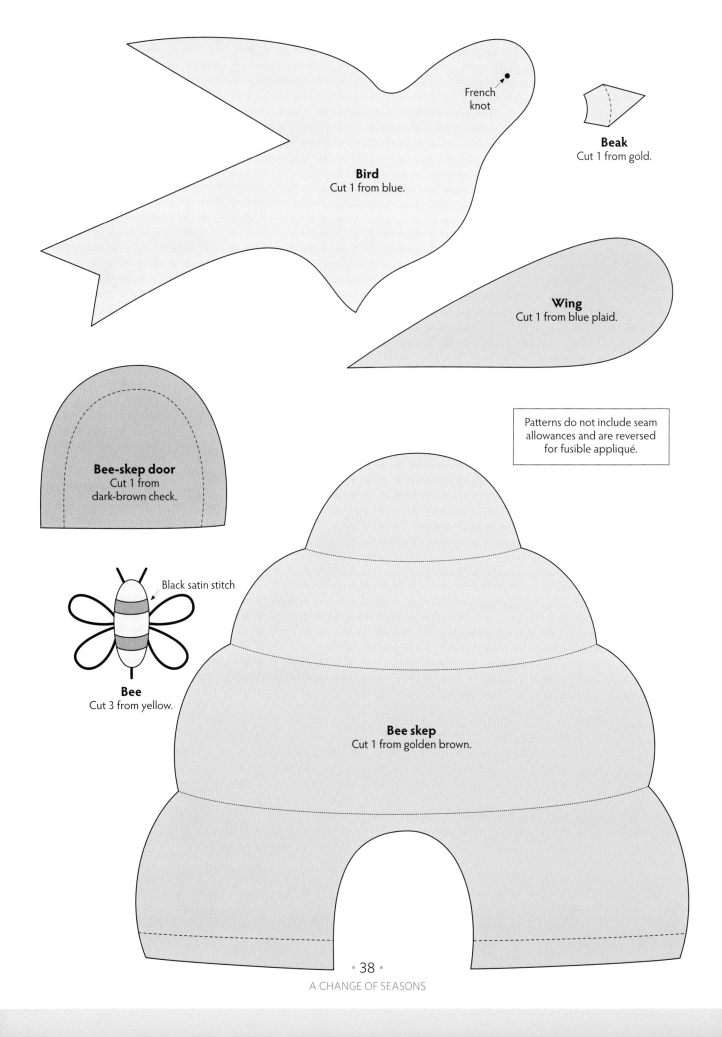

French knot

Bird
Cut 1 from blue.

Beak
Cut 1 from gold.

Wing
Cut 1 from blue plaid.

Bee-skep door
Cut 1 from
dark-brown check.

Patterns do not include seam
allowances and are reversed
for fusible appliqué.

Black satin stitch

Bee
Cut 3 from yellow.

Bee skep
Cut 1 from golden brown.

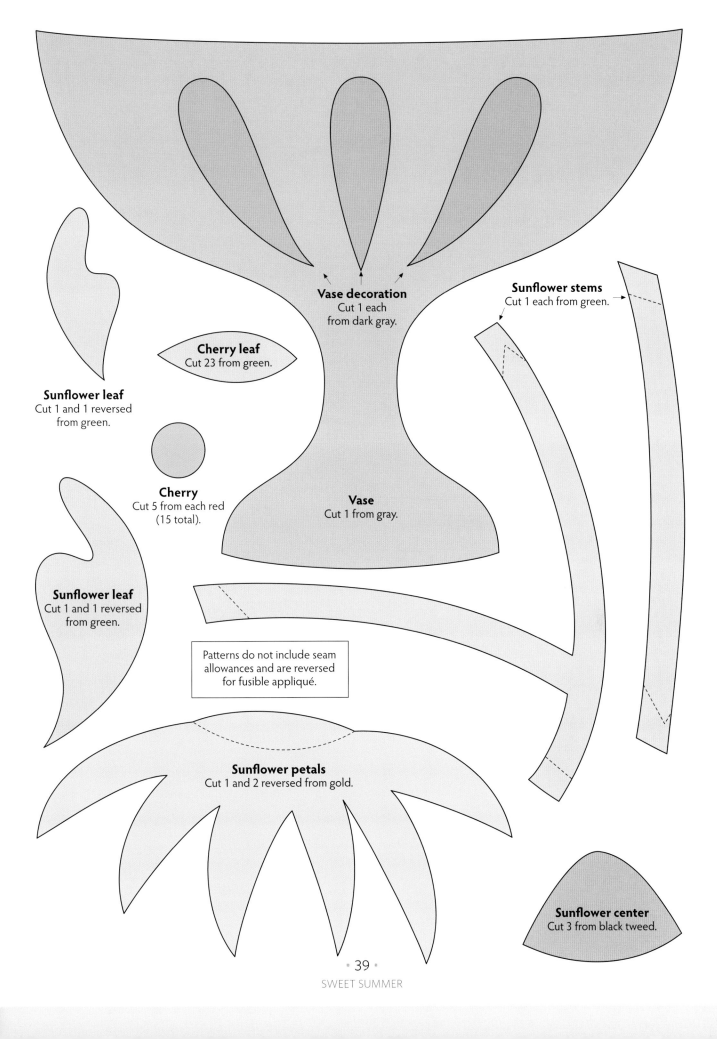

Vase decoration
Cut 1 each
from dark gray.

Sunflower stems
Cut 1 each from green.

Cherry leaf
Cut 23 from green.

Sunflower leaf
Cut 1 and 1 reversed
from green.

Cherry
Cut 5 from each red
(15 total).

Vase
Cut 1 from gray.

Sunflower leaf
Cut 1 and 1 reversed
from green.

Patterns do not include seam
allowances and are reversed
for fusible appliqué.

Sunflower petals
Cut 1 and 2 reversed from gold.

Sunflower center
Cut 3 from black tweed.

Summer Celebration

designed by BONNIE SULLIVAN, pieced by MARJORIE McCANSE,
appliquéd by BONNIE SULLIVAN, and quilted by PAM PARVIN

The sweet fruits of summer make this quilt festive. The red print with black polka dots reminds me of a juicy watermelon—and echoes the watermelon appliqués.

FINISHED SIZE: 48" x 48"
FINISHED CENTER BLOCK: 20" x 20"

FLANNEL

Yardage is based on 42"-wide flannel fabric.

1½ yards of red-with-black polka dots for star border, outer border, and binding
¾ yard of tan plaid for block background
⅔ yard of oatmeal tweed for appliqué background
⅜ yard *each* of 2 assorted green plaids for checkerboard borders
1 fat quarter (18" x 21") *each* of 3 assorted red prints and/or plaids for star border

WOOL

All wool sizes are for felted wool.

7" x 12" rectangle of red for watermelon and cherries
2" x 3" rectangle *each* of 2 different reds for cherries
2½" x 18" rectangle of green for watermelon rind and cherry leaves
6" x 8" rectangle of olive green for sunflower stems, leaves, and cherry leaves
8" x 22" rectangle of white for watermelon and dogtooth border
11" x 14" rectangle of blue for birds
4" x 9" rectangle of blue plaid for birds' wings
9" x 10" rectangle of gold for sunflowers, bee, and birds' beaks
3½" x 4" rectangle of dark brown/black tweed for sunflower centers

OTHER MATERIALS

3¼ yards of fabric for backing
54" x 54" piece of batting
1⅛ yards of 18"-wide lightweight, paper-backed fusible web
Thread to match wool colors
White thread for watermelon seeds
Removable marking pen (such as a Frixion pen)
11 black buttons, ¼" diameter, for watermelon seeds
Freezer paper

PEARL COTTON

Colors listed below are for Valdani pearl cotton. See "Resources" on page 111.

Olive Green for cherry branches
Tarnished Gold for cherry stems and birds' legs and feet
Black for birds' eyes and bee details

CUTTING

From the oatmeal tweed, cut:
1 square, 21" x 21"

From *each* of the red fat quarters, cut:*
24 squares, 2½" x 2½" (72 total)

*After cutting, label one stack of 24 matching squares as A, label a second stack of 24 matching squares as B, and label the remaining 24 squares as C.

Continued on page 42

Continued from page 40

From *each* of the green plaids, cut:
4 strips, 2½" x 42" (8 total)

From the tan plaid, cut:
1 strip, 6½" x 42"; crosscut into:
    4 squares, 6½" x 6½"
    8 squares, 2½" x 2½"
3 strips, 4½" x 42"; crosscut into:
    8 squares, 4½" x 4½"
    28 rectangles, 2½" x 4½"

From the red-with-black polka dots, cut:
7 strips, 4½" x 42"; crosscut *2 of the strips* into
    12 squares, 4½" x 4½"
    5 strips, 2½" x 42"

APPLIQUÉING THE CENTER BLOCK

Refer to "Working with Wool" on page 107 for detailed information. See "Decorative Stitches" on page 110 as needed.

1. From the olive-green wool, cut four ⅜" x 4" strips for the sunflower stems. From the green wool, cut one ⅜" x 18" strip for the rind of the watermelon.

2. Using the patterns on pages 47–49, trace each appliqué shape the number of times indicated on the pattern onto the paper side of the fusible web. Cut out each shape about ⅛" outside the drawn lines. See "Trace to Fit" on page 107.

3. Following the manufacturer's instructions, fuse each shape, glue side down, onto the wrong side

of the designated wool color. Cut out each shape exactly on the drawn lines.

4. Using the dogtooth pattern on page 49 and extending the section to 16 points, trace one section onto the unwaxed side of the freezer paper. Press the shiny side of the section onto the white wool, placing the section along one edge of the wool. Cut out the section exactly on the drawn lines.

5. Using the photo on page 42 as a guide and starting with the watermelon and petals, arrange the appliqué pieces on the oatmeal tweed square. Pin the stems in place, curving them as shown. Note that you'll need to tuck some pieces under another piece, such as the top part of the half sunflower under the half-sunflower center.

Align the edge of the watermelon rind strip with the edge of the watermelon piece, bending the strip to the desired shape. Trim the strip to the required length and pin the watermelon rind in place. Position the white dogtooth strip along the inside edge of the rind, curving the strip as needed. Pin the strip in place. Note that the background square will be trimmed in step 10; be sure to keep all of the appliqué pieces at least 1" from the outer edges of the square on all sides.

Use a removable marking pen to mark the cherry branches to make leaf placement easier. I use a Frixion pen to mark the branches. The lines from the Frixion pen will disappear when you iron the pieces in place. *Do not* use a water-soluble marker, as the heat of the iron will permanently set the lines. Fuse the appliqué pieces to the background.

6. Using thread that matches the wool appliqués, whipstitch the pieces in place.

7. Use green pearl cotton and two rows of outline stitching for the cherry branches.

8. Use gold pearl cotton and outline stitching for the stems of the cherries. Using gold pearl cotton, embroider two rows of outline stitching for the birds' legs and one row of outline stitching for the birds' feet.

9. Using black pearl cotton, make French knots for the birds' eyes. Use black pearl cotton and straight stitches for the bee's antennae and stinger, a satin stitch for the stripes on the bee, and lazy daisy stitches for the bee's wings.

10. Press the appliquéd block and trim it to 20½" x 20½", keeping the design centered.

MAKING THE CHECKERBOARD BORDERS

1. Sew two different green strips together as shown to make a strip set. Press the seam allowances open. Make four strip sets. Crosscut the strip sets into 60 segments, 2½" wide.

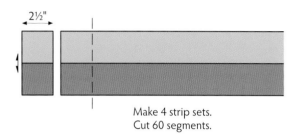

Make 4 strip sets.
Cut 60 segments.

2. Sew five segments together to make a 20½"-long strip. Sew six segments together to make a 24½"-long strip. Sew nine segments together to make a 36½"-long strip. Sew 10 segments together to make a 40½"-long strip. Press all seam allowances open. Make two of each strip.

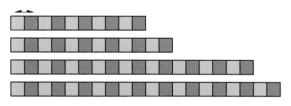

Make 2 of each.

MAKING THE STAR BORDER

1. Draw a diagonal line from corner to corner on the wrong side of each red 2½" square. Place a marked square on one end of a tan-plaid 2½" x 4½" rectangle, right sides together and raw edges aligned. Stitch along the marked line. Trim away the excess fabrics, leaving a ¼" seam allowance. Press the seam allowances open to reduce bulk. Place a different red square on the

other end of the rectangle as shown. Sew, trim, and press to make a flying-geese unit. Make the number of flying-geese units indicated of each fabric combination.

Make 12.   Make 4 of each.

2. Using the remaining marked red squares, place a red square on one corner of a tan-plaid 4½" square, right sides together and raw edges aligned. Stitch along the marked line. Trim away the excess fabrics, leaving a ¼" seam allowance. Press the seam allowances open to reduce bulk. In the same way, sew red squares on the remaining three corners of the tan-plaid square as shown. Make eight square-in-a-square units.

Make 8.

3. Lay out five flying-geese units, two square-in-a-square units, two tan-plaid 2½" squares, two tan-plaid 2½" x 4½" rectangles, and three red-with-black dots 4½" squares as shown. Join the pieces to make a strip. Press the seam allowances open. Make four strips.

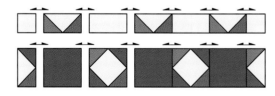

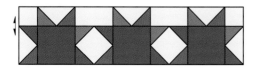

Make 4.

ASSEMBLING THE QUILT TOP

1. Sew the green 20½"-long strips to opposite sides of the center block. Press the seam allowances open. Sew the green 24½"-long strips to the top and bottom of the block. Press the seam allowances open.

2. Sew star-border strips to opposite sides of the quilt top. Press the seam allowances open. Sew tan-plaid 6½" squares to both ends of the two remaining star-border strips. Press the seam allowances open. Sew these strips to the top and bottom of the quilt top. Press the seam allowances open.

3. Sew the green 36½"-long strips to opposite sides of the center block. Press the seam allowances open. Sew the green 40½"-long strips to the top and bottom of the block. Press the seam allowances open.

4. Join the red-with-black dots 4½"-wide strips end to end. From the pieced strip, cut two 40½"-long strips and two 48½"-long strips. Sew the 40½"-long strips to opposite sides of the quilt top. Press the seam allowances open. Sew the 48½"-long strips to the top and bottom of the quilt top to complete the outer border. Press the seam allowances open.

Quilt assembly

5. Referring to the photos above and on page 43, fuse a bird and berry on each of the four corners of the quilt top. Using thread that matches the wool appliqués, whipstitch the pieces in place.

6. Using black pearl cotton, make French knots for the birds' eyes.

7. Use gold pearl cotton and an outline stitch to stitch the stems of the cherries.

8. For the dogtooth-border sections, extend the dogtooth pattern on page 49 to 20 points (or teeth!) long. Trace four extended rows next to each other onto the paper side of the fusible web as shown. Cut the sections apart on the drawn lines. Then cut on the traced zigzag lines to make eight sections.

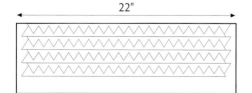

22"

9. Place the white dogtooth sections on top of the red-with-black dots outer border, aligning the straight edge of the dogteeth with the green pieced border as shown on page 43 and overlapping the ends as needed. Fuse, and then whipstitch the dogtooth sections in place using white thread.

FINISHING

For more details on any of the following steps, go to ShopMartingale.com/HowtoQuilt for free, downloadable information.

1. Layer the quilt top with batting and backing; baste the layers together.

2. Machine quilt as desired. Trim the batting and backing so the edges are even with the quilt top.

3. Use the red-with-black dots 2½"-wide strips to make and attach binding.

4. Using white thread, sew the black buttons to the watermelon for seeds.

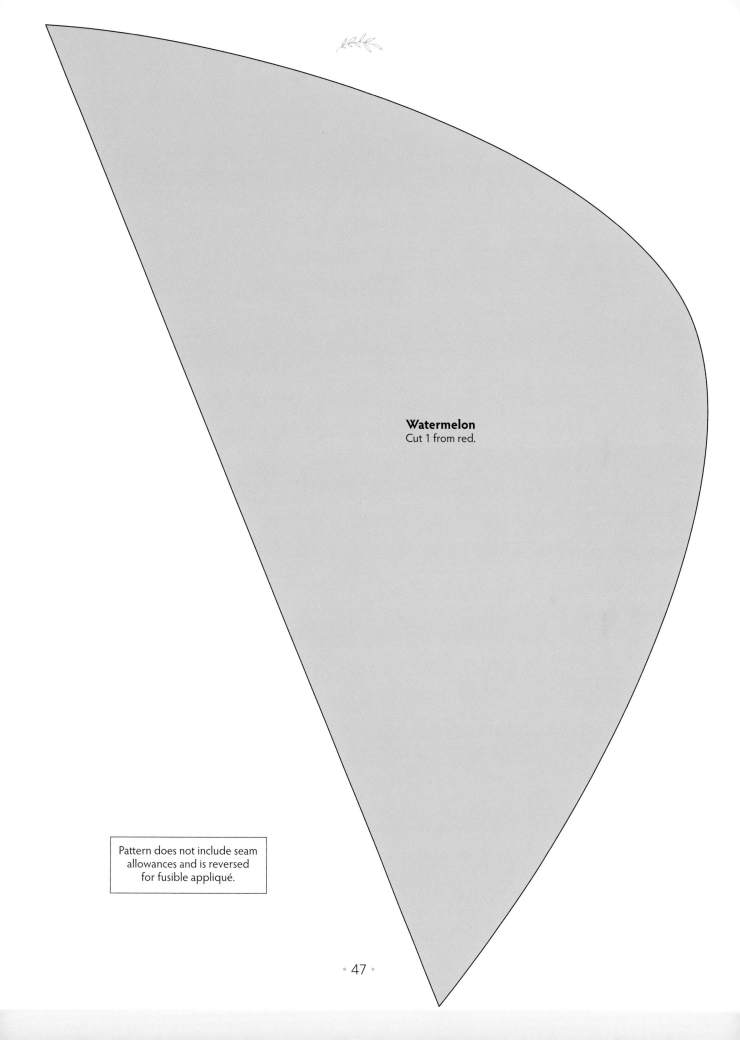

Watermelon
Cut 1 from red.

Pattern does not include seam allowances and is reversed for fusible appliqué.

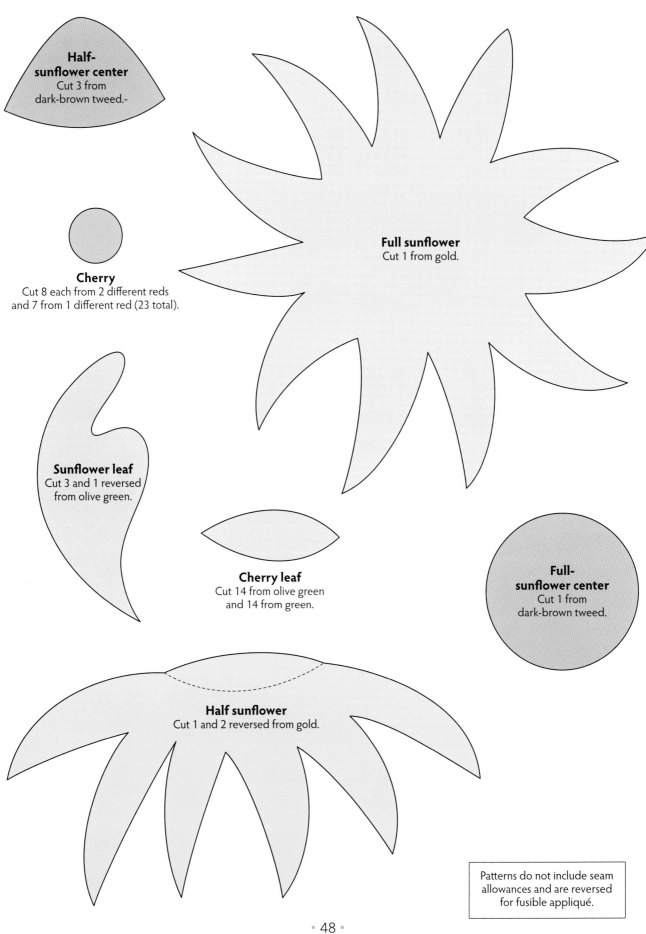

Half-sunflower center
Cut 3 from dark-brown tweed.-

Cherry
Cut 8 each from 2 different reds and 7 from 1 different red (23 total).

Full sunflower
Cut 1 from gold.

Sunflower leaf
Cut 3 and 1 reversed from olive green.

Cherry leaf
Cut 14 from olive green and 14 from green.

Full-sunflower center
Cut 1 from dark-brown tweed.

Half sunflower
Cut 1 and 2 reversed from gold.

Patterns do not include seam allowances and are reversed for fusible appliqué.

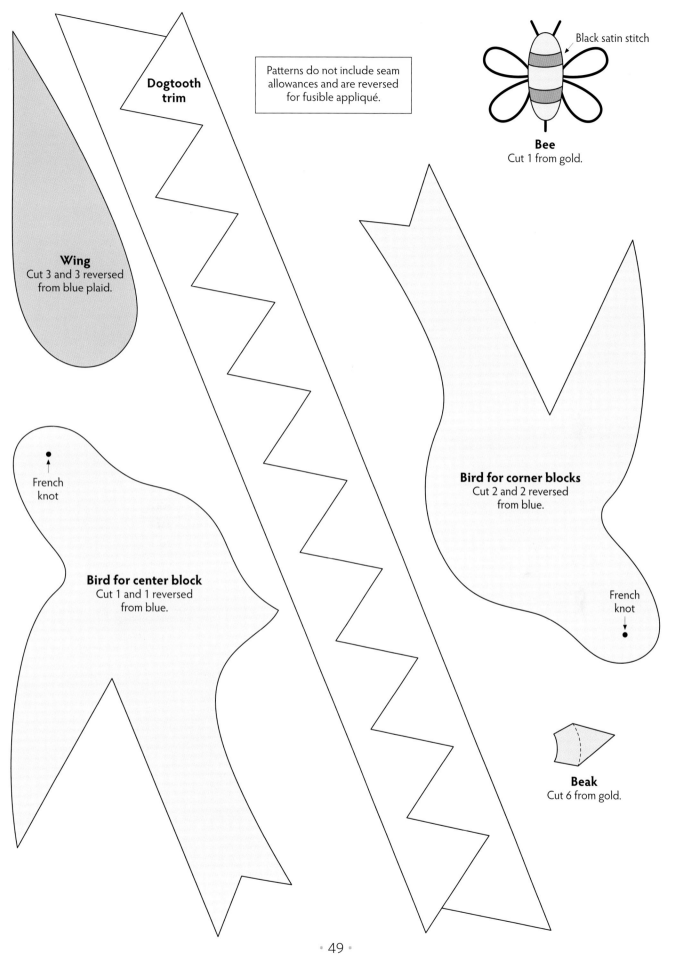

Dogtooth trim

Patterns do not include seam allowances and are reversed for fusible appliqué.

Black satin stitch

Bee
Cut 1 from gold.

Wing
Cut 3 and 3 reversed from blue plaid.

Bird for corner blocks
Cut 2 and 2 reversed from blue.

French knot

French knot

Bird for center block
Cut 1 and 1 reversed from blue.

Beak
Cut 6 from gold.

Watermelon Banner

designed and made by BONNIE SULLIVAN

*Imagine this banner hanging at your next family get-together—
or adorning the table at a summer picnic.*

FINISHED SIZE: 36" long x 7½" tall, including ties

MATERIALS

*All wool sizes are for felted wool. Flannel yardage is
based on 42"-wide fabric.*

¼ yard of red-with-black polka dots for watermelon
    pennants
1 strip, 2½" x 42", of green houndstooth flannel
    for ties
4" x 8" rectangle of white wool for zigzag trim
2 white buttons, ⅝" diameter, for hanging loops
White thread
Black heavy-duty thread
Freezer paper

ASSEMBLING THE BANNER

1. Fold the ¼ yard of red-with-black dots in half,
   right sides together. Trace the triangle pattern
   on page 53 onto the unwaxed side of the freezer
   paper. Cut out the freezer-paper template. Use
   the template to trace five triangles onto the
   fabric, as shown. Cut out the triangles to make
   five triangle pairs (10 triangles total).

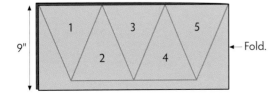

2. With right sides still together, sew along the two
   long sides of a triangle pair, leaving the top open
   for turning. Clip the excess fabric from the point.
   Turn the triangles right side out and press. Trim
   the tiny dog-ears that extend beyond the top
   edge as shown. Make five watermelon pennants.

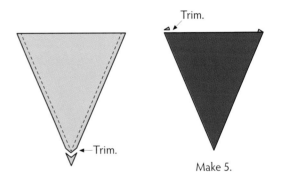

Make 5.

Sewing Strong Points

To ensure that your points are secure, shorten
the stitch length about 1" before and after each
point. Then use a blunt object, such as a
chopstick, to push out the point when turning
the pennant right side out.

3. Trace the zigzag trim pattern on page 53 three times onto the unwaxed side of freezer paper. Press the shiny side of the freezer paper onto the white wool. Cut out each pattern exactly on the drawn lines. Then cut each pattern apart on the zigzag line to make two six-point units. You'll need five six-points units; one will be extra.

4. Lay a white zigzag strip along the top edge of each watermelon pennant with the straight edge of the strip about ⅛" down from the top of the pennant. Pin in place. Using white thread,

machine or hand baste the straight edge of the zigzag strip to the watermelon pennant as shown. Whipstitch the zigzag points to the pennant. Make five.

Make 5.

5. Press the green flannel strip in half lengthwise, wrong sides together. Center the watermelon pennants along the raw edge of the the green strip as shown, leaving an equal amount of strip on each end. Pin the pennants in place. Using a ⅜" seam allowance, sew the pennants to the strip.

6. Fold the strip over the top of the watermelon pennants, making sure to cover the line of stitching. On each end of the strip, fold over ⅜" to the wrong side. Topstitch along the entire length of the tie, stitching as close to the folded edge as possible.

7. On one end, fold the end of the tie to the back of the strip to make a 3" loop for hanging. Using black heavy-duty thread, sew a white button on the front of the banner, catching the ends on the back to secure the loop in place. Repeat on the other end of the tie.

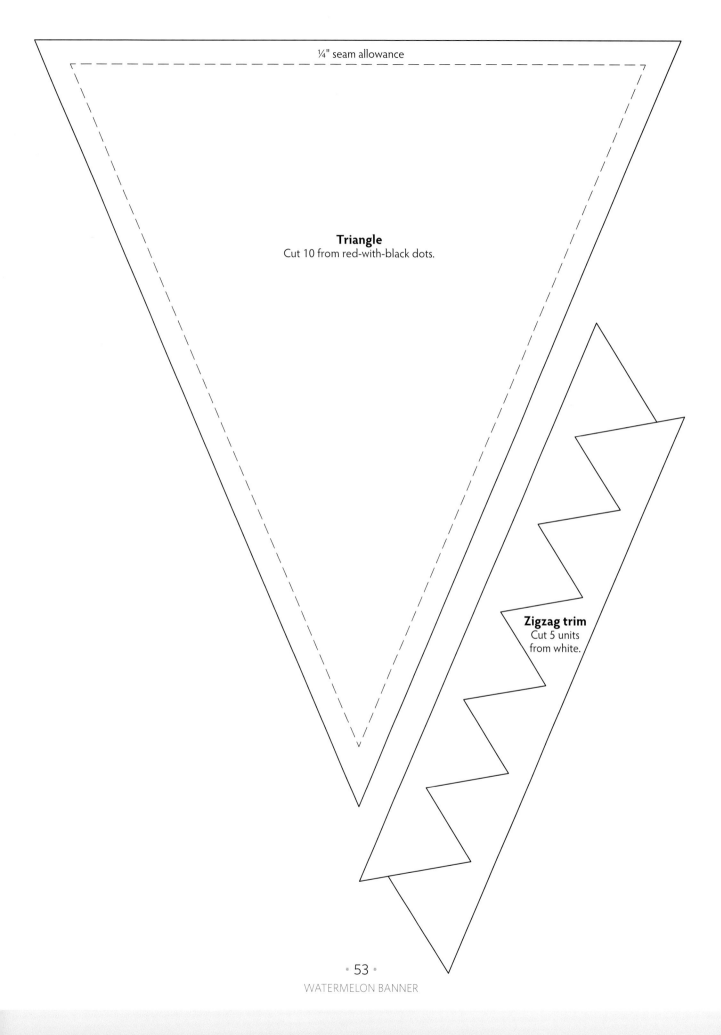

¼" seam allowance

Triangle
Cut 10 from red-with-black dots.

Zigzag trim
Cut 5 units
from white.

Sunflowers

designed and made by BONNIE SULLIVAN

The stems of these sunflowers are made from tape-wrapped wire, so you can bend them around anything. Brighten up unexpected places with a sunny blossom!

FINISHED BLOSSOM: 4" diameter

WOOL

All wool sizes are for felted wool. Yields 1 Sunflower.

4½" x 9" rectangle of gold for sunflower petals*
3½" x 3½" square of brown tweed for sunflower center

OTHER MATERIALS

1 covered-button blank, 2" diameter, with slightly rounded top
1 brown two-holed button, 1" diameter, with slight curve or lip
Thread to match gold wool
18" length of green floral wire
Green floral tape
Glue gun with glue sticks
Freezer paper

*I used both gold and orange wool for the sunflower petals.

ASSEMBLING THE SUNFLOWER

1. Using the patterns on page 57 and the freezer-paper method described on page 108, trace each shape the number of times indicated on the pattern onto the unwaxed side of the freezer paper.

2. Press the shiny side of each shape onto the right side of the designated fabric. Cut out each shape exactly on the lines.

3. Following the manufacturer's instructions, cover the button-cover blank with the circle of brown tweed wool.

4. Center the covered button on one of the sunflower petals. Using a coordinating color of thread and pulling the petals slightly toward the front of the flower, sew a running stitch on the wrong side of the sunflower where the petals meet the edge of the covered button, making sure to catch the wool on the button as you stitch.

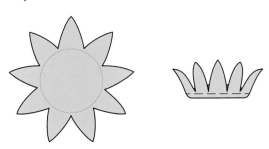

5. Place the second sunflower petal on the back of the first one, offsetting it so the petals show between the petals of the first sunflower. Using a minimal amount of hot glue, glue the second sunflower in place. Try to avoid having any glue showing and be sure to cover the stitched line from step 4. Do not place glue at the center of the sunflower back.

6. Cut a very small slit in the center on the back of the two sunflower petals, just big enough to push the covered button shank through. Thread the floral wire through the shank to the center of the wire. Bend the wire in half. Insert the ends of the wire through the holes in the brown button. The side of the button with the rim should be facing the back of the sunflower so the

button fits snugly and hides the shank. Push the button up to the back of the sunflower. Twist the two wires tightly at the top to hold the button in place, and then twist them together all the way to the ends. Cover the entire stem with green floral tape for a cleaner look.

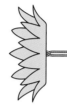

Tips for Floral Tape

Floral tape isn't sticky until you stretch it. You need to stretch the tape while simultaneously wrapping it around the wire stem. To start, use your thumb to hold the floral tape in place. While holding the tape in place, quickly wrap the floral tape tightly around the wire stem three or four times. Continue to gently stretch and wrap the tape down the wire. ⟳

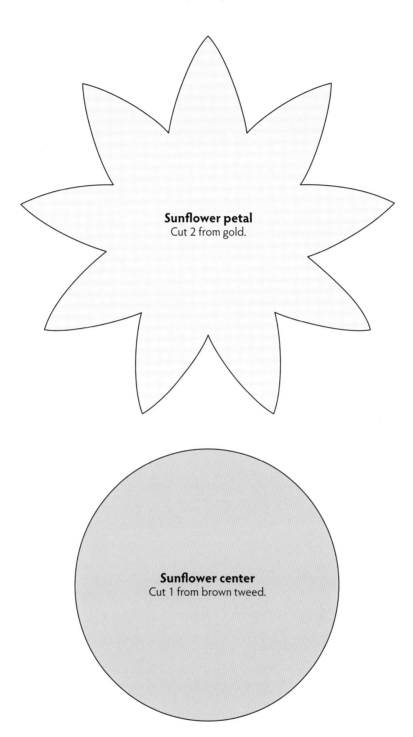

Sunflower petal
Cut 2 from gold.

Sunflower center
Cut 1 from brown tweed.

Patterns do not include
seam allowances.

Harvest Home

designed and made by BONNIE SULLIVAN

*Acorns and pears are the season's harvest, and an
autumn pumpkin makes a happy home for a crow.*

FINISHED SIZE: 23" x 19", framed

LINEN

20" x 24" rectangle of linen for background (see
"Background Fabric" on page 6 for details)

WOOL

All wool sizes are for felted wool.

5½" x 10" rectangle of gray plaid for vase

5" x 7" rectangle of orange for pumpkin

6" x 7" rectangle of green plaid (A) for leaves and
pumpkin stem

5" x 6" rectangle of green plaid (B) for leaves

5" x 6" rectangle of light green (C) for leaves

2½" x 7" rectangle of dark gray for crow

3" x 4½" rectangle of black for crow's wing and
pumpkin door

2" x 3½" rectangle of gold for pumpkin windows

4" x 4" square of orange gold for pears

1½" x 6" rectangle of brown for branches

3" x 3" square of light brown for acorns

1" x 5" rectangle of medium brown herringbone or
tweed for acorn caps

1½" x 7½" rectangle of white for vase trim

2" x 2" square of red for berries

OTHER MATERIALS

½ yard of 18"-wide lightweight, paper-backed
fusible web

Thread to match wool colors

Removable marking pen (such as a Frixion pen)

19" x 23" frame, with a 16" x 20" interior opening

16" x 20" piece of foam-core board

PEARL COTTON

*Colors listed below are for Valdani pearl cotton.
See "Resources" on page 111.*

Aged Black (charcoal) for pumpkin windows

Black for crow's leg and foot

Olive Green for leaves and tendrils

Rusted Orange for pumpkin lines

Tarnished Gold for pear stems

Coffee Roast (dark brown) for acorn stems

PREPARING THE APPLIQUÉS

Refer to "Working with Wool" on page 107 for
detailed information.

1. From the brown wool, cut one ⅜" x 5½" strip
    and two ⅜" x 4" strips for the branches. See
    "Trace to Fit" on page 107.

2. Using the patterns on pages 62 and 63, trace
    each appliqué shape the number of times
    indicated on the pattern onto the paper side of
    the fusible web. Cut out each shape about ⅛"
    outside the drawn lines.

3. Following the manufacturer's instructions, fuse each shape, glue side down, to the wrong side of the designated wool color. Cut out each shape exactly on the drawn lines.

APPLIQUÉING THE DESIGN

See "Decorative Stitches" on page 110 as needed.

1. To mark a 16" x 20" rectangle on the linen rectangle, lay the piece of cardboard or glass that came with the frame in the center of the rectangle. Using a pencil, carefully trace all around the cardboard or glass. The marked rectangle is your design boundary; be sure to keep your design within the lines. (See "Use a Basting Line" on page 9 for an optional way to mark the design boundary.)

2. Using the photo above as a guide and starting with the vase and pumpkin, arrange the appliqué pieces on the background. Pin the branches in place, curving them as shown. Note that you'll need to tuck some pieces under another piece, such as the bottom of the pumpkin under the vase. Fuse the appliqué pieces to the background.

3. Using thread that matches the wool appliqués, whipstitch the pieces in place.

4. Using black pearl cotton, outline stitch around the windows and embroider the pane definition in the center of the windows as shown in the photo at right. Using black pearl cotton, outline stitch the crow's leg and foot.

5. Using green pearl cotton, outline stitch the veins and stems of the leaves. I also stitched the vein along the edge of the half-leaves. Outline stitch the curly pumpkin tendrils. You can use a removable marking pen to mark the tendrils before stitching. I use a Frixion pen to mark the tendrils. The lines from the Frixion pen will disappear when ironed. *Do not* use a water-soluble marker as the heat of the iron will permanently set the lines.

6. Using orange pearl cotton, outline stitch the definition lines on the pumpkin.

7. Use gold pearl cotton and two rows of outline stitching for the stems on the pears.

8. Use brown pearl cotton and two rows of outline stitching for the stems on the acorns.

FINISHING

Place the foam-core board on the wrong side of the embroidered piece, centering the stitched design. Fold the edges of the fabric over the foam-core board, making sure the fabric is taut but not distorted. Secure the fabric with tape and then insert the backing into the frame and secure with the clips that came with the frame.

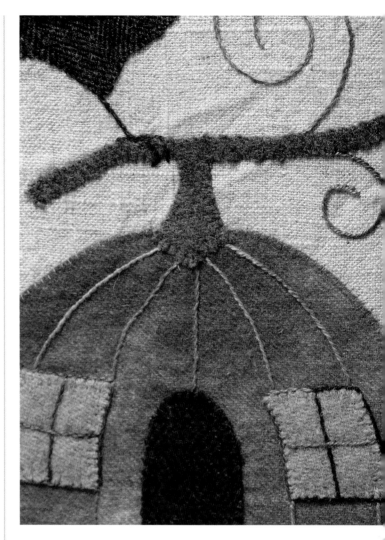

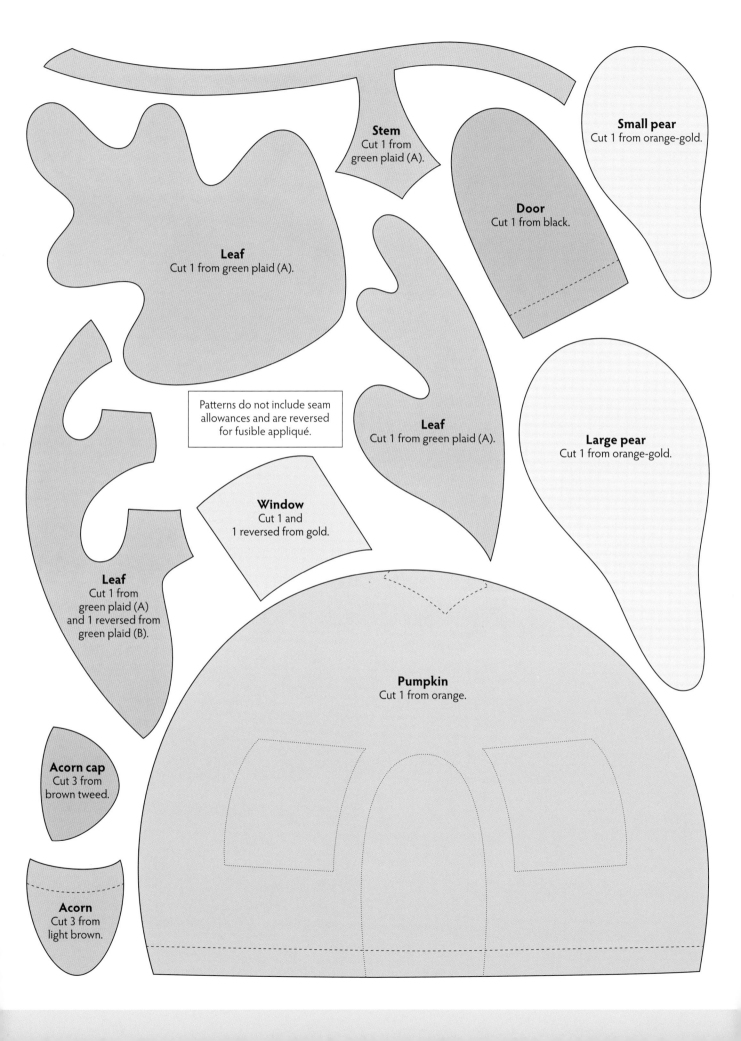

Stem
Cut 1 from
green plaid (A).

Leaf
Cut 1 from green plaid (A).

Door
Cut 1 from black.

Small pear
Cut 1 from orange-gold.

Patterns do not include seam
allowances and are reversed
for fusible appliqué.

Leaf
Cut 1 from green plaid (A).

Large pear
Cut 1 from orange-gold.

Window
Cut 1 and
1 reversed from gold.

Leaf
Cut 1 from
green plaid (A)
and 1 reversed from
green plaid (B).

Pumpkin
Cut 1 from orange.

Acorn cap
Cut 3 from
brown tweed.

Acorn
Cut 3 from
light brown.

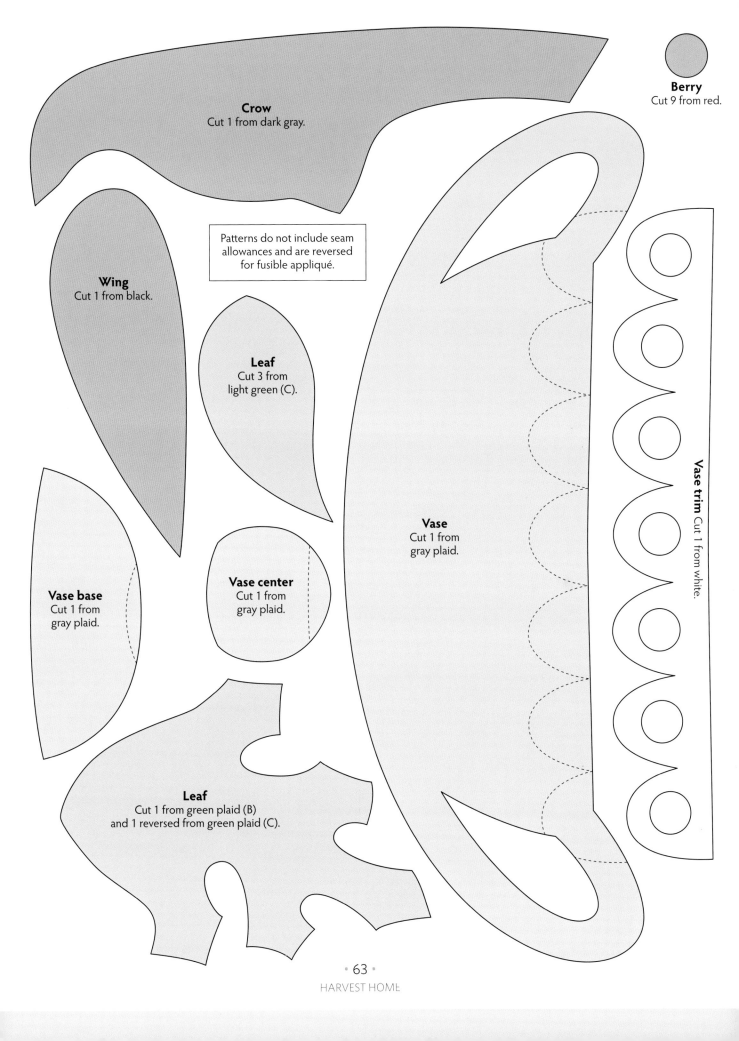

Berry
Cut 9 from red.

Crow
Cut 1 from dark gray.

Patterns do not include seam allowances and are reversed for fusible appliqué.

Wing
Cut 1 from black.

Leaf
Cut 3 from light green (C).

Vase
Cut 1 from gray plaid.

Vase trim Cut 1 from white.

Vase base
Cut 1 from gray plaid.

Vase center
Cut 1 from gray plaid.

Leaf
Cut 1 from green plaid (B) and 1 reversed from green plaid (C).

Autumn Star

designed by BONNIE SULLIVAN, pieced by SHARON GIFFORD and BONNIE SULLIVAN,
appliquéd by BONNIE SULLIVAN, and quilted by PAM PARVIN

Rich colors and appliquéd acorns make this a cozy quilt for cuddling under on fall nights.

FINISHED SIZE: 48½" x 48½"
FINISHED BLOCK: 6" x 6"

FLANNEL

Yardage is based on 42"-wide flannel fabric.

1¼ yards of black plaid for appliqué background
8 fat quarters (18" x 21") of assorted autumn prints
    and plaids for blocks*
½ yard of black-with-brown dots for binding

*I used orange plaid, orange-with-black dots, dark-green plaid, brown herringbone, brown-and-black herringbone, green bouclé, gold tweed, and black-with-brown dots.

WOOL

All wool sizes are for felted wool.

12" x 12" square *each* of 4 different greens for leaves
3" x 27" strip of brown for branches and stems
8" x 9" rectangle of light brown for acorns
6" x 9" rectangle of brown tweed for acorn caps
2" x 3" rectangle *each* of 3 different reds or rusts
    for berries
8" x 9" rectangle of gold for star

OTHER MATERIALS

3¼ yards of fabric for backing
54" x 54" piece of batting
1⅛ yards of 18"-wide lightweight, paper-backed
    fusible web
Thread to match wool colors

PEARL COTTON

*Colors listed below are for Valdani pearl cotton.
See "Resources" on page 111.*

Olive Green for leaf veins and stems
Coffee Roast (dark brown) for acorn stems

CUTTING

From the black plaid, cut:
1 square, 25" x 25"
4 squares, 13" x 13"

From *each* autumn fat quarter, cut:
4 strips, 3" x 21"; crosscut into 24 squares, 3" x 3"
    (192 total)
2 strips, 2½" x 21"; crosscut into 12 squares,
    2½" x 2½" (96 total)

From the black-with-brown dots, cut:
6 strips, 2½" x 42"

MAKING THE APPLIQUÉ BLOCKS

Refer to "Working with Wool" on page 107 for detailed information. See "Decorative Stitches" on page 110 as needed.

1. For the branches and stems, cut five ⅜" x 27"
    strips from the brown wool. Cut the strips into
    the following pieces:
    -   2 strips, ⅜" x 26"
    -   4 strips, ⅜" x 9"
    -   4 strips, ⅜" x 4½"
    -   4 strips, ⅜" x 2"

2. Using the patterns on page 69, trace each appliqué shape the number of times indicated on the pattern onto the paper side of the fusible web. Cut out each shape about ⅛" outside the drawn lines.

3. Following the manufacturer's instructions, fuse each shape, glue side down, onto the wrong side of the designated wool color. Cut out each shape exactly on the drawn lines.

4. Using the photos above and on page 67 as a guide and starting with the branches and stems, arrange the appliqué pieces in the center of the black-plaid squares. Pin the stems in place, curving them as shown. Note that you'll need to tuck some pieces under another piece, such as the top of the acorn under the acorn cap. Fuse the appliqué pieces to the background. The background squares are slightly oversized and will be trimmed in step 8. Make one center block and four corner blocks.

5. Using thread that matches the wool appliqués, whipstitch the pieces in place.

6. Using green pearl cotton, outline stitch the veins and stems of the leaves.

7. Use brown pearl cotton and two rows of outline stitching for the stems on the acorns.

8. Trim the appliquéd center block to 24½" x 24½", keeping the design centered. Trim each corner block to 12½" x 12½", again keeping the design centered.

MAKING THE DOUBLE X BLOCKS

1. From each of the autumn colors, make four piles consisting of three 3" squares and three 2½" squares, all matching. Draw a diagonal line from corner to corner on the wrong side of each of the 3" squares.

2. Using a different autumn color, randomly add three 3" squares to each pile, so that each pile consists of three 3" squares from two different colors. You should have 32 piles of squares.

3. Using the 3" squares from one pile, layer different 3" squares right sides together with the marked square on top. Sew ¼" from each side of the marked line. Cut the squares apart on the drawn line. Press the seam allowances open to reduce bulk. Trim the half-square-triangle unit to measure 2½" x 2½". Repeat to make six units from each pile of squares.

4. Lay out six identical half-square-triangle units and three matching 2½" squares in three rows as shown. Join the pieces into rows. Press the seam allowances open. Join the rows and press the seam allowances open. Repeat to make 32 Double X blocks that measure 6½" square.

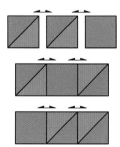
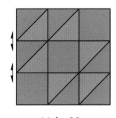

Make 32.

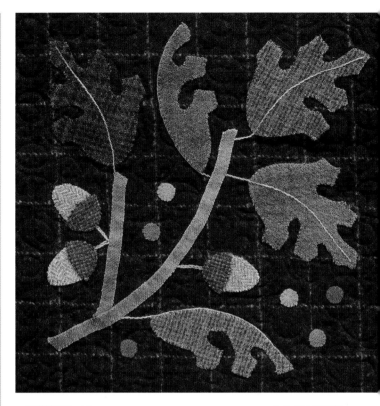

ASSEMBLING THE QUILT TOP

1. Randomly lay out two rows of four Double X blocks each as shown in the quilt assembly diagram below. Join the blocks into rows. Press the seam allowances open. Join the rows and press the seam allowances open. Make two horizontal rows and two vertical rows.

2. Lay out the block rows from step 1 and the appliquéd blocks as shown in the quilt assembly diagram. Join the pieces into rows. Press the seam allowances open. Join the rows and press the seam allowances open.

FINISHING

For more details on any of the following steps, go to ShopMartingale.com/HowtoQuilt for free, downloadable information.

1. Layer the quilt top with batting and backing; baste the layers together.

2. Machine quilt as desired. Trim the batting and backing so the edges are even with the quilt top.

3. Use the black-with-brown dots 2½"-wide strips to make and attach binding.

Quilt assembly

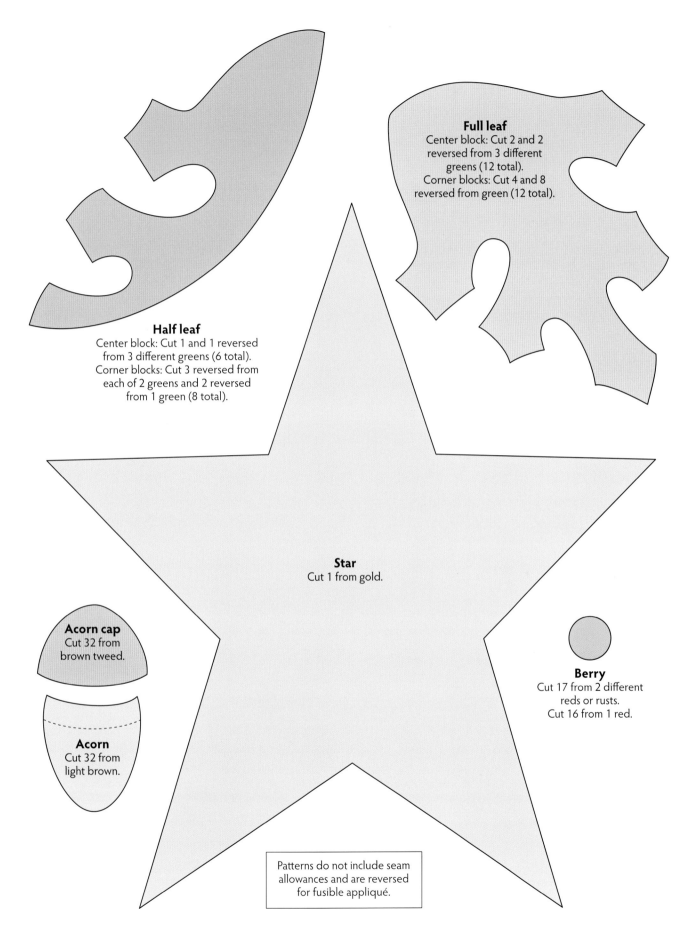

Full leaf
Center block: Cut 2 and 2 reversed from 3 different greens (12 total).
Corner blocks: Cut 4 and 8 reversed from green (12 total).

Half leaf
Center block: Cut 1 and 1 reversed from 3 different greens (6 total).
Corner blocks: Cut 3 reversed from each of 2 greens and 2 reversed from 1 green (8 total).

Star
Cut 1 from gold.

Acorn cap
Cut 32 from brown tweed.

Acorn
Cut 32 from light brown.

Berry
Cut 17 from 2 different reds or rusts.
Cut 16 from 1 red.

Patterns do not include seam allowances and are reversed for fusible appliqué.

Dance of the Autumn Leaves

designed and made by BONNIE SULLIVAN

Dreary fall days turn festive when you hang this banner.
Whimsical acorn people will bring smiles to any fall celebration.

FINISHED BANNER: 8" x 33", including hanging loops

FLANNEL

Yardage is based on 42"-wide flannel fabric.

⅜ yard of green plaid for backing and tie
⅓ yard of tan-and-cream stripe for background

WOOL

All wool sizes are for felted wool.

4" x 4" square *each* of 5 different autumn colors for
  leaves*
3" x 4" rectangle of light brown for acorns
3" x 3" square of brown herringbone or tweed for
  acorn caps
1½" x 1½" square *each* of 3 different rusts or reds for
  berries

I used 2 rust plaids, 2 green plaids, and 1 gold plaid.

OTHER MATERIALS

½ yard of 18"-wide lightweight, paper-backed
  fusible web
Thread to match wool colors
Black heavy-duty thread
6 off-white buttons, ½" to ⅝" diameter, for tie
Freezer paper
Frixion pen (optional)

PEARL COTTON

Color listed below is for Valdani pearl cotton.
See "Resources" on page 111.

Black for leaf veins, arms, legs, and facial features

CUTTING

From the green plaid flannel, cut:
1 strip, 2½" x 42"
1 strip, 8½" x 42"

APPLIQUÉING THE PENNANTS

Refer to "Working with Wool" on page 107 for
detailed information. See "Decorative Stitches"
on page 110 as needed.

1. Trace the pennant pattern on page 73 onto the
   unwaxed side of the freezer paper. Cut out the
   freezer-paper template. Use the template to
   trace five pennants onto the tan-and-cream
   stripe. Cut out the pennants on the traced line.
   Make five.

2. Use the template to trace five pennants onto the
   green-plaid 8½"-wide strip. Cut out the
   pennants on the traced line. Make five.

3. Using the Autumn Star patterns on page 69,
   trace five acorns, five acorn caps, 10 berries, and
   five full leaves onto the paper side of the fusible
   web, making sure to reverse three leaves. Cut
   out each shape about ⅛" outside the drawn lines.

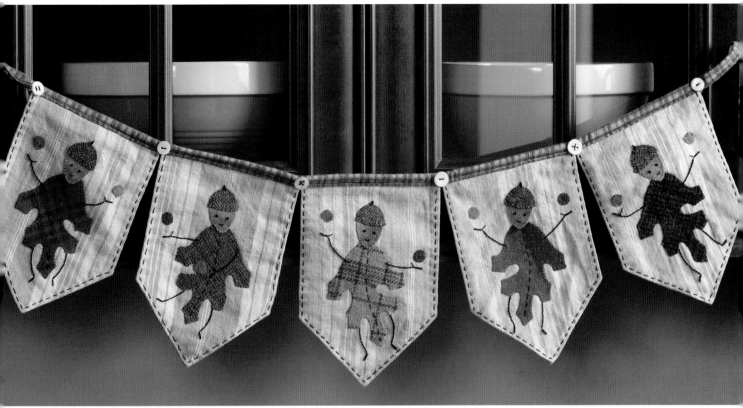

4. Following the manufacturer's instructions, fuse each shape, glue side down, onto the following wool colors. Make five light-brown acorns and five brown acorn caps. Using a mix of the three different rust/red wools, make 10 berries. Using a mix of the five different autumn-colored wools, make two leaves and three reversed leaves. Cut out each shape exactly on the drawn lines.

5. Using the photos above and at right as guides, arrange one acorn, one acorn cap, one leaf, and two berries on one pennant. Note that you'll need to tuck some pieces under another piece, such as the top of the leaf under the acorn. Fuse the appliqué pieces to the background.

6. Using thread that matches the wool appliqués, whipstitch the pieces in place.

7. Using black pearl cotton and a running stitch, embroider a vein through the center of each leaf. Using black pearl cotton, outline stitch the arms and legs, making sure to keep the toes and

fingers at least ½" from the outer edges. (You can stitch these freehand but if you'd feel more comfortable, use a Frixion pen to draw them first.) Use two straight stitches for the fingers and feet. Use one stitch for the thumbs. Use two or three small straight stitches for the top of the acorn cap. Make two small straight stitches in the form of a shallow V for the mouth. Stitch a French knot for each eye.

ASSEMBLING THE BANNER

1. Layer one appliquéd pennant and one green-plaid pennant, right sides together, and sew down one side, along the bottom edges, and up the other side using a ¼" seam allowance. Leave the top open for turning. Clip the excess fabric from the point. Turn the pennants right side out and press. Make five.

Make 5.

2. Using black pearl cotton, sew a running stitch a generous ⅛" from the edge of each pennant as shown. Do not sew along the top edge.

3. Press the green-plaid strip in half lengthwise, wrong sides together. Center the pennants along the raw edges of the green strip as shown, leaving an equal amount of strip on each end. Pin the pennants in place. Using a ⅜" seam allowance, sew the pennants to the strip.

4. Fold the strip over the top of the pennants, making sure to cover the line of stitching. On each end of the strip, fold over ⅜" to the wrong side. Topstitch along the entire length of the tie, stitching as close to the folded edge as possible.

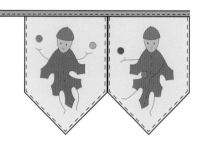

5. Fold one end of the tie to the back of the strip to make a 3" loop for hanging. Using black heavy-duty thread, sew an off-white button to the front of the banner, catching the ends on the back to secure the loop in place. Repeat on the other end of the tie. Sew off-white buttons on the front of the banner between the individual pennants as shown.

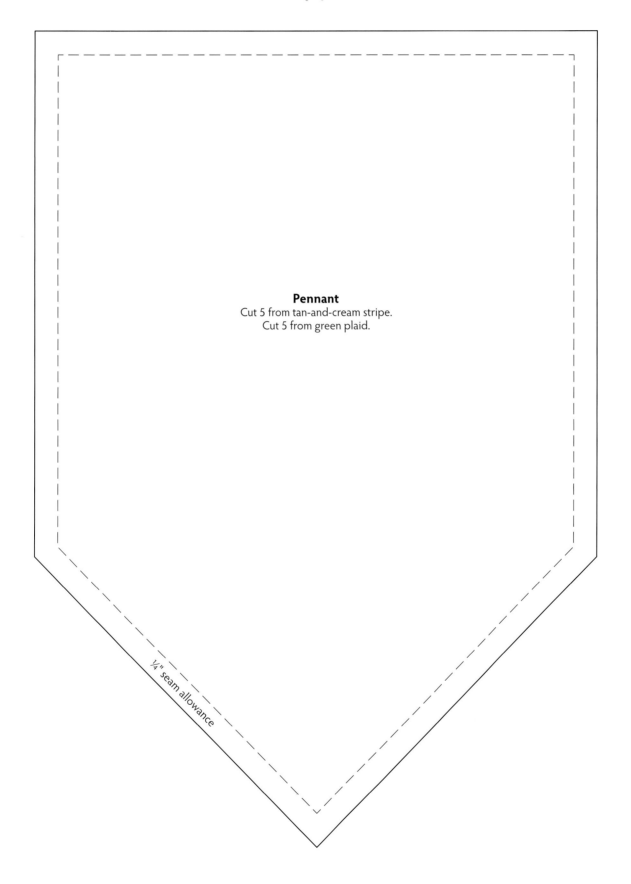

Pennant
Cut 5 from tan-and-cream stripe.
Cut 5 from green plaid.

¼" seam allowance

Autumn Crow

designed and made by BONNIE SULLIVAN

What crow wouldn't want a dapper acorn necklace?
Perched on a candlestick, he's ready to show off.

FINISHED CROW BODY: 5" tall x 10" long

MATERIALS

All wool sizes are for felted wool.

12" x 19" rectangle of black wool for crow
4" x 14" rectangle of black-with-brown dots
    flannel for wing lining
Polyester fiberfill for stuffing
2 black beads, ⅛" diameter, for eyes
Black heavy-duty thread
Wooden candlestick, 6½" tall
18" length of green ribbon (optional)
Acorn for embellishment (optional)
Heavy-duty wire and permanent glue
    (such as E-6000)
Freezer paper
Drill

ASSEMBLING THE CROW

Use a ¼" seam allowance throughout.

1. Using the patterns on pages 76 and 77 and the freezer-paper method described on page 108, trace each shape the number of times indicated on the pattern onto the unwaxed side of the freezer paper.

2. Press the shiny side of each shape onto the right side of the designated wool color. Cut out each shape exactly on the drawn lines.

3. Place a crow's body and the belly right sides together, aligning the dots. Sew the pieces together from the dots to the end of the tail.

Align the second crow's body with the other side of the belly and sew the pieces together from the dots to the tail.

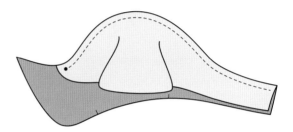

4. Sew the two bodies together from the dot to the end of the tail, leaving an opening in the middle of the back for turning.

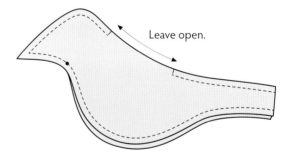

Leave open.

5. Flatten the end of the tail so that the seam along the back of the crow is centered and sew across the end of the tail.

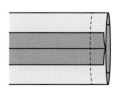

6. Trim the excess wool at the corners of the tail and around the beak. Clip the curves. Turn the crow right side out through the opening. Stuff the crow with polyester fiberfill. Close the opening with a slip stitch.

7. Layer a black-wool wing and a black-with-brown dots wing right sides together. Sew all the way around the wings. Trim the excess wool from the pointed end of the wing and around the curved end. On the underside of the wing, make a slit in the center of the wing. Turn the wing right side out through the slit. Press and whipstitch the slit closed. (You don't have to be too neat, as the slit will not show.) Repeat to make a second wing.

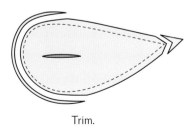

Trim.

8. Machine stitch parallel lines on each wing. Position a wing on each side of the crow as shown in the photo on page 75. Pin the wings in place. On each side, whipstitch the front half of the wing in place. If you want, you can tack the wing tips to the tail as well.

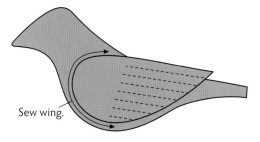

Sew wing.

9. Using black heavy-duty thread, sew a bead on each side of the crow's head, pulling on the thread to make a slight indentation where the eyes will be.

10. Drill a small hole through an acorn and hang it around the crow's neck with a green ribbon. Trim each end of the ribbon on the diagonal. Or, embellish your crow however you wish.

11. Using a drill bit that's about the same diameter as the heavy-duty wire, drill a hole into the center of the candlestick. See "Wooden Candlestick" on page 32. Insert a small, firm wire into the hole so that about 2" of the wire extends above the rim of the candlestick holder. Glue the wire in place. When dry, insert the wire into the underbelly of the crow to hold it in place.

¼" seam allowance

Flip on dashed line to complete pattern.

Crow belly
Cut 1 from black.

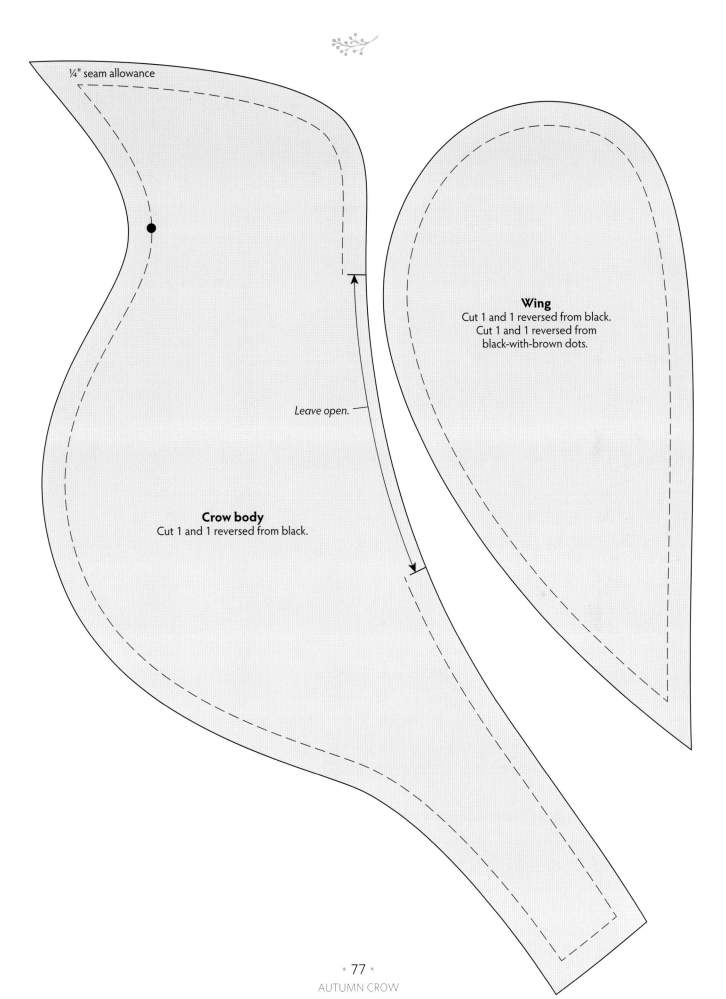

¼" seam allowance

Crow body
Cut 1 and 1 reversed from black.

Leave open.

Wing
Cut 1 and 1 reversed from black.
Cut 1 and 1 reversed from
black-with-brown dots.

Winter Wonders

designed and made by BONNIE SULLIVAN

The mittens were hung on the holly branches with care...
and stuffed with peppermint sticks!

FINISHED SIZE: 23" x 19", framed

LINEN

20" x 24" piece of linen for background (see
"Background Fabric" on page 6 for details)

WOOL

All wool sizes are for felted wool.

5" x 5" square of red for bird and wing
1½" x 9½" rectangle of light red for cake-stand top
3½" x 4½" rectangle of medium-red plaid for cake-
    stand base
4" x 4" square of dark red for cake-stand base and
    holly berries
4" x 7½" rectangle of brown for holly branches and
    snowman's twig arm
7" x 11" rectangle of green for holly leaves
4½" x 6" rectangle of blue plaid for mittens
4" x 5" rectangle of dark-teal check for scarf
5" x 9" rectangle of white for snowman and candy
    canes
1" x 1½" rectangle of orange for carrot nose
1" x 1" square of gold for bird's beak
2" x 2½" rectangle of light green for mistletoe leaves

OTHER MATERIALS

½ yard of 18"-wide lightweight, paper-backed
    fusible web
2 two-holed black buttons, ¼" diameter, for
    snowman's eyes
5 white buttons, ¼" diameter, for mistletoe berries

Thread to match wool colors
Black and white thread to attach buttons
19" x 23" frame, with a 16" x 20" interior opening
16" x 20" piece of foam-core board

PEARL COTTON

Colors listed below are for Valdani pearl cotton. See
"Resources" on page 111.

Withered Green for holly leaf veins and stem and
    mistletoe stem
Old Brick (dark red) for candy cane stripes
Tarnished Gold for bird's leg and foot
Aged Black (charcoal) for mittens' hanging loops
Black for bird's eye
White for snowflakes

PREPARING THE APPLIQUÉS

Refer to "Working with Wool" on page 107 for
detailed information.

1. Using the patterns on pages 82 and 83, trace
    each appliqué shape the number of times
    indicated on the pattern onto the paper side of
    the fusible web. Cut out each shape about ⅛"
    outside the drawn lines. See "Trace to Fit" on
    page 107.

2. Following the manufacturer's instructions, fuse
    each shape, glue side down, onto the wrong side
    of the designated wool color. Cut out each shape
    exactly on the drawn lines.

APPLIQUÉING THE DESIGN

See "Decorative Stitches" on page 110 as needed.

1. To mark a 16" x 20" rectangle on the linen rectangle, lay the piece of cardboard or glass that came with the frame in the center of the rectangle. Using a pencil, carefully trace all around the cardboard or glass. The marked rectangle is your design boundary; be sure to keep your design within the lines. (See "Use a

Basting Line" on page 9 for an optional way to mark the design boundary.)

2. Using the photo above as a guide and starting with the cake stand and snowman, arrange the appliqué pieces on the background. Note that you'll need to tuck some pieces under another piece, such as the bottom of the snowman under the cake stand. Fuse the appliqué pieces to the background.

3. Using thread that matches the wool appliqués, whipstitch the pieces in place.

4. Using green pearl cotton, outline stitch the stem of the mistletoe sprig and the holly leaves' veins and stems.

5. Use red pearl cotton to embroider the stripes on the candy canes as shown in the photo.

6. Using gold pearl cotton, embroider two rows of outline stitching for the bird's leg and one row of outline stitching for the bird's foot.

7. Use black pearl cotton to make a French knot for the bird's eye.

8. Use aged-black pearl cotton and an outline stitch to make the hanging loops for the mittens.

9. Use white pearl cotton and a variety of stitches, including an outline stitch, straight stitches, French knots, and daisy stitches, to stitch the snowflakes as shown in the photo. The patterns are at right.

10. Use black thread to sew on the white buttons for the mistletoe berries.

11. Use white thread to sew on the black buttons for the snowman's eyes as shown in the photo.

FINISHING

Place the foam-core board on the wrong side of the embroidered piece, centering the stitched design. Fold the edges of the fabric over the foam-core board, making sure the fabric is taut but not distorted. Tape the fabric in place. Insert the backing into the frame and secure it with the clips that came with the frame.

Transferring the Snowflake Patterns

Use a light box and a removable marking pen to trace the snowflake patterns onto the appliquéd rectangle. If you don't have a light box, you can tape the design to a window or use a glass-topped table with a lamp underneath. ✍

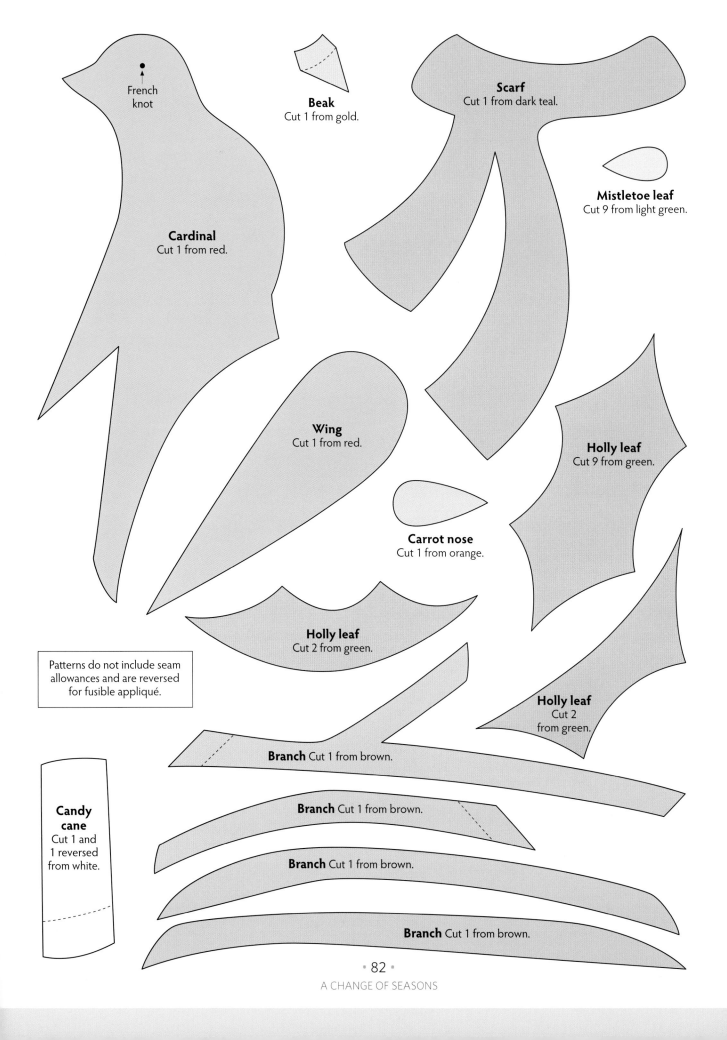

French knot

Beak
Cut 1 from gold.

Scarf
Cut 1 from dark teal.

Mistletoe leaf
Cut 9 from light green.

Cardinal
Cut 1 from red.

Wing
Cut 1 from red.

Holly leaf
Cut 9 from green.

Carrot nose
Cut 1 from orange.

Holly leaf
Cut 2 from green.

Patterns do not include seam allowances and are reversed for fusible appliqué.

Holly leaf
Cut 2
from green.

Branch Cut 1 from brown.

Branch Cut 1 from brown.

Candy cane
Cut 1 and 1 reversed from white.

Branch Cut 1 from brown.

Branch Cut 1 from brown.

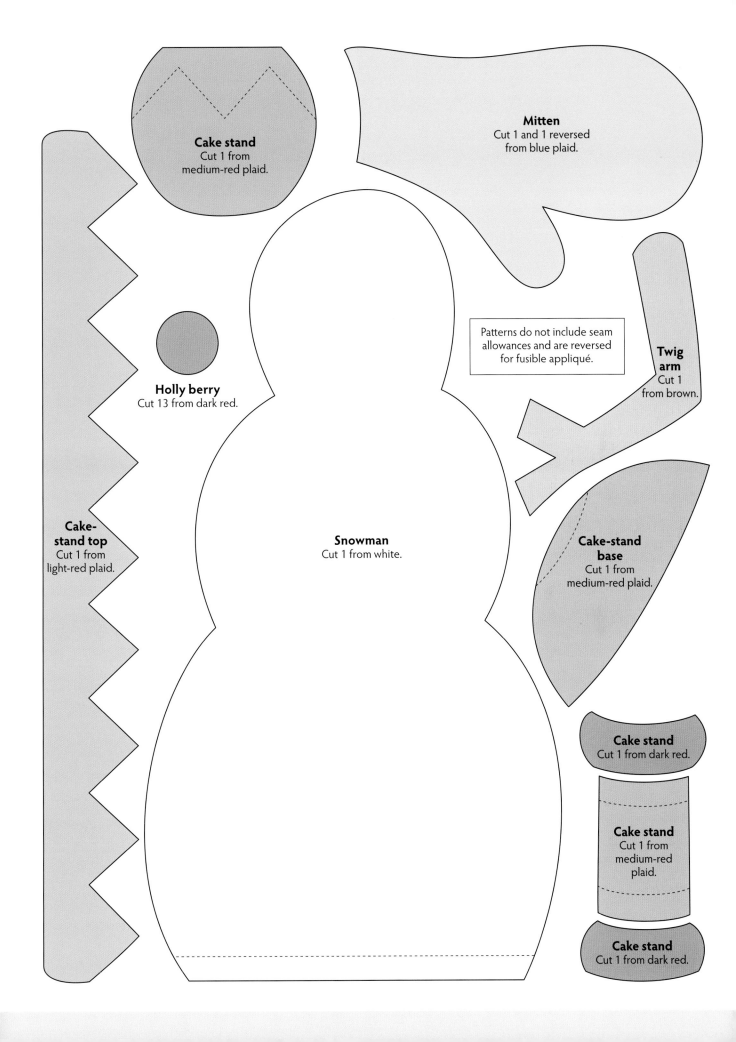

Cake stand
Cut 1 from
medium-red plaid.

Mitten
Cut 1 and 1 reversed
from blue plaid.

Holly berry
Cut 13 from dark red.

Patterns do not include seam
allowances and are reversed
for fusible appliqué.

Twig arm
Cut 1
from brown.

Cake-stand top
Cut 1 from
light-red plaid.

Snowman
Cut 1 from white.

Cake-stand base
Cut 1 from
medium-red plaid.

Cake stand
Cut 1 from dark red.

Cake stand
Cut 1 from
medium-red
plaid.

Cake stand
Cut 1 from dark red.

Holly in My Heart

designed by BONNIE SULLIVAN, pieced and appliquéd by MARJORIE McCANSE, and quilted by PAM PARVIN

Symbols of nature and love combine in a fabulous holiday quilt.
Use a variety of reds for a pretty, scrappy effect.

FINISHED SIZE: 56½" x 56½"
FINISHED BLOCK: 12" x 12"

FLANNEL

Yardage is based on 42"-wide flannel fabric.

2 yards of espresso check for appliqué background, outer border, and binding
8 fat quarters (18" x 21") of greens for blocks*
8 fat quarters of red plaids and prints for blocks*
1¾ yards of tan print for blocks

Label the green fat quarters 1–8. Label the red fat quarters A–H.

WOOL

All wool sizes are for felted wool.

6" x 11" rectangle *each* of 3 greens for holly leaves
5" x 8" rectangle *each* of 4 reds for hearts
2" x 9" rectangle of brown for holly branches

OTHER MATERIALS

3¾ yards of fabric for backing
62" x 62" piece of batting
⅞ yard of 18"-wide lightweight, paper-backed fusible web
Thread to match wool colors

PEARL COTTON

Colors listed below are for Valdani pearl cotton. See "Resources" on page 111.

Withered Green for holly leaf veins
Black for hearts

CUTTING

From *each* of the 8 red fat quarters, cut:
2 strips, 3" x 21"; crosscut into 11 squares, 3" x 3" (88 total)
3 strips, 2½" x 21"; crosscut into 21 squares, 2½" x 2½" (168 total)

From *each* of the 8 green fat quarters, cut:
3 strips, 4½" x 21"; crosscut into 9 squares, 4½" x 4½" (72 total)

From the tan print, cut:
11 strips, 4½" x 42"; crosscut into:
    40 squares, 4½" x 4½"
    105 rectangles, 2½" x 4½"
3 strips, 2½" x 42"; crosscut into:
    3 rectangles, 2½" x 4½"
    36 squares, 2½" x 2½"

From the espresso check, cut:
2 strips, 12½" x 42"; crosscut into:
    4 squares, 12½" x 12½"
    5 rectangles, 4½" x 12½"
4 strips, 4½" x 42"; crosscut into:
    3 rectangles, 4½" x 12½"
    12 rectangles, 4½" x 8½"
    4 squares, 4½" x 4½"
7 strips, 2½" x 42"

MAKING THE STAR BLOCKS

1. Draw a diagonal line from corner to corner on the wrong side of each red A, B, D, and G 3" square. Layer a marked A square right sides

together with a red H 3" square. Sew ¼" from each side of the marked line. Cut the squares apart on the drawn line. Press the seam allowances open to reduce bulk. Make 22 A/H half-square-triangle units. Trim the units to measure 2½" x 2½". Repeat to make 22 B/C units, 22 D/E units, and 22 G/F units.

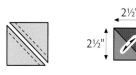

Make 22 of each.

2. Using one unit of each fabric combination, assemble a pinwheel unit. Press the seam allowances open. Make 21 units. You'll have one half-square-triangle unit of each fabric combination left over.

Make 21.

3. Draw a diagonal line from corner to corner on the wrong side of each red 2½" square. Place a marked A square on one end of a tan rectangle, right sides together and raw edges aligned. Stitch along the marked line. Trim away the excess fabrics, leaving a ¼" seam allowance. Press the seam allowances open to reduce bulk. Place a marked B square on the other end of the rectangle as shown above right. Sew, trim, and press to make a flying-geese unit. Make 15 units of each fabric combination. Set aside the remaining marked red squares for step 1 of "Making the Sashing Units."

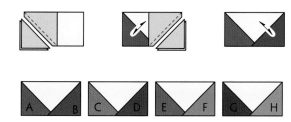

Make 15 of each.

4. Lay out one pinwheel unit from step 2, one of each flying-geese unit from step 3, and four tan 2½" squares, making sure that the reds in the flying-geese units match the adjoining triangles in the pinwheel unit. Join the units into rows. Press the seam allowances open. Join the rows to make a Star block. Press the seam allowances open. Make nine blocks.

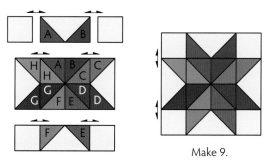

Make 9.

5. Join the remaining flying-geese units to the pinwheel units as shown, matching the adjoining triangle colors. Make six of each partial-star unit.

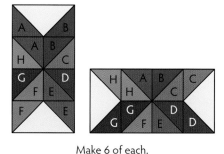

Make 6 of each.

MAKING THE SASHING UNITS

1. Place a marked red A square on one corner of a tan 4½" square, right sides together and raw edges aligned. Stitch along the marked line. Trim away the excess fabrics, leaving a ¼" seam allowance. Press the seam allowances open to

reduce bulk. Place a marked red B square on an adjacent corner of the tan-with-black square. Sew, trim, and press to make a unit as shown. Make six units of each fabric combination.

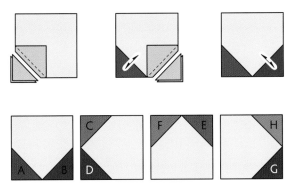

Make 6 of each.

2. Sew tan rectangles to opposite sides of a unit from step 1 as shown. Press the seam allowances open. Make six of each unit.

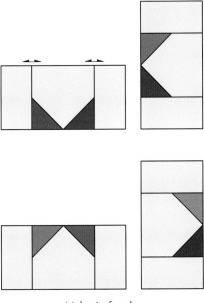

Make 6 of each.

3. Draw a diagonal line from corner to corner on the wrong side of each green square. Place a marked green #6 square on one corner of a unit from step 2, right sides together and raw edges aligned. Stitch along the marked line. Trim away the excess fabrics, leaving a ¼" seam allowance. Press the seam allowances toward the resulting

green triangle. Place a marked green #5 square on an adjacent corner of the unit. Sew, trim, and press to make a star-point unit. Make six units of each fabric combination.

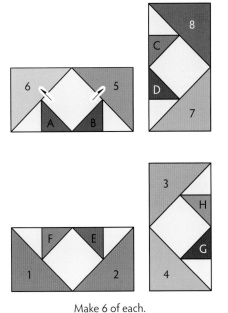

Make 6 of each.

4. Lay out one partial-star unit and two units from step 3 as shown, making sure to match the adjoining triangle colors. Join the units and press the seam allowances open. Make six units of each.

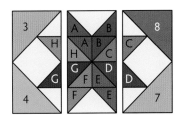

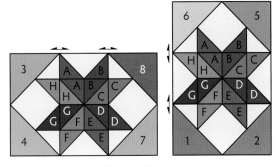

Make 6 of each.

MAKING THE BORDER UNITS

Repeat step 3 of "Making the Star Blocks" on page 86 using the remaining marked green squares and the espresso 4½" x 8½" rectangles. Make three units of each fabric combination.

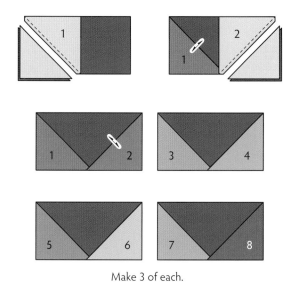

Make 3 of each.

MAKING THE APPLIQUÉD BLOCKS

Refer to "Working with Wool" on page 107 for detailed information. See "Decorative Stitches" on page 110 as needed.

1. Using the patterns on page 91, trace each appliqué shape the number of times indicated on the pattern onto the paper side of the fusible web. Cut out each shape about ⅛" outside the drawn lines. See "Trace to Fit" on page 107 for a time-saving tip.

2. Following the manufacturer's instructions, fuse each shape, glue side down, onto the wrong side of the designated wool color. Cut out each shape exactly on the drawn lines.

3. Using the photo on page 89 as a guide and starting with the heart, arrange the appliqué pieces on the espresso 12½" squares. Notice in the center of the heart, a holly branch section is stitched on top of the heart. Be sure to keep the section aligned with the other ends of the branches, which are tucked under the edges of

the heart. Fuse the appliqué pieces to the background. Make two with the branch and leaves pointed in one direction as shown, and two with the branch and leaves pointed in the opposite direction.

4. Using thread that matches the wool appliqués, whipstitch the pieces in place.

5. Using black pearl cotton, sew a running stitch around the heart, about ¼" from the edge of the heart.

6. Using green pearl cotton, outline stitch the veins on the holly leaves.

7. Draw a diagonal line from corner to corner on the wrong side of each tan 4½" square. Place marked squares on opposite corners of an appliquéd block, right sides together and raw edges aligned. Stitch along the marked line. Trim away the excess fabrics, leaving a ¼" seam allowance. Press the seam allowances open to reduce bulk. Place marked squares on the two remaining corners as shown. Sew, trim, and press to make an appliquéd snowball block. Make two of each unit.

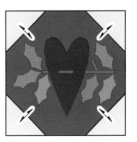 

Make 2 of each.

ASSEMBLING THE QUILT TOP

Refer to the quilt assembly diagram below throughout. After sewing each seam, press the seam allowances open.

1. To make the top row, join two espresso 4½" squares, three border units, and two espresso 4½" x 12½" rectangles. Repeat to make the bottom row.

2. To make a Star block row, join two border units, three Star blocks, and two horizontal sashing units. Make three rows.

3. To make an appliquéd block row, join two espresso 4½" x 12½" rectangles, three vertical sashing units, and two appliquéd blocks with the branches and leaves pointing to the right. Make a second row with the branches and leaves in both blocks pointing to the left.

4. Sew the rows together. Press the seam allowances open.

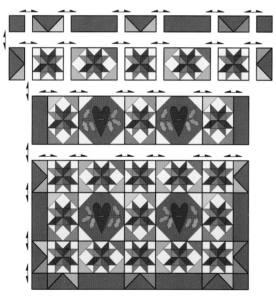

Quilt assembly

FINISHING

For more details on any of the following steps, go to ShopMartingale.com/HowtoQuilt for free, downloadable information.

1. Layer the quilt top with batting and backing; baste the layers together.

2. Machine quilt as desired. Trim the batting and backing so the edges are even with the quilt top.

3. Use the espresso 2½"-wide strips to make and attach binding.

Change It Up

Here's an idea for a different block for this quilt. Use the cardinal and holly leaf from the Winter Wonders pattern on page 82. For the holly branch, use a brown wool ⅜"-wide strip. Curve the strip to shape and cut it to length. Embellish with red buttons for holly berries.

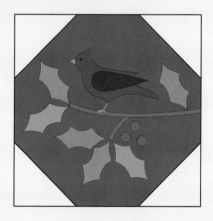

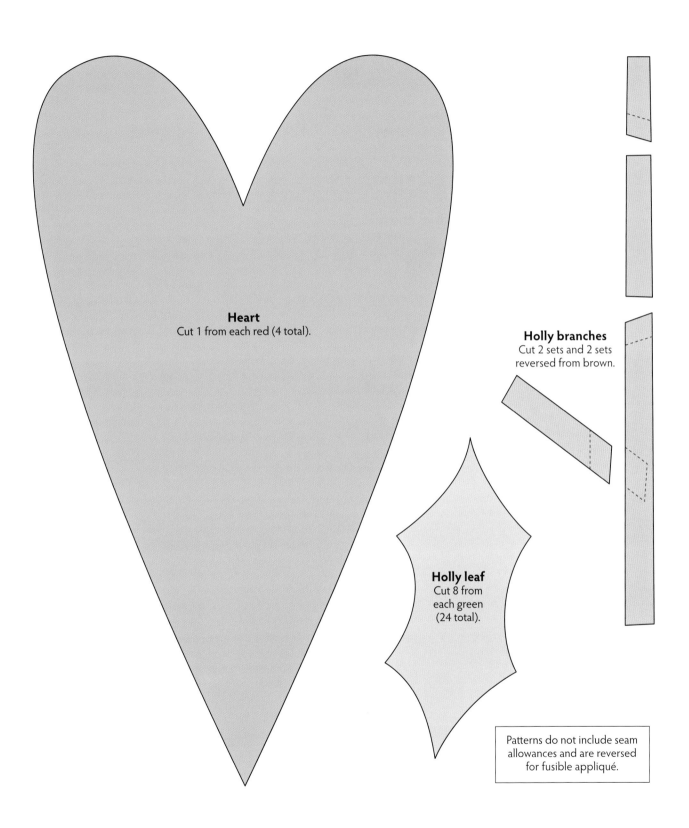

Heart
Cut 1 from each red (4 total).

Holly branches
Cut 2 sets and 2 sets
reversed from brown.

Holly leaf
Cut 8 from
each green
(24 total).

Patterns do not include seam
allowances and are reversed
for fusible appliqué.

The Stockings Were Hung

designed and made by BONNIE SULLIVAN

Peace, joy, love, and noël: Convey holiday wishes with homemade stockings.

FINISHED SIZE: 9½" x 21½"
YIELDS 4 STOCKINGS

FLANNEL AND LINEN

Cotton yardage is based on 42"-wide flannel fabric.

1½ yards of red-print flannel for lining of stockings

6 fat quarters (18" x 21") of assorted dark flannels (black, dark brown, and gray) for patchwork

¾ yard of dark-gray herringbone flannel for back of stockings

¼ yard of cream linen for stocking cuffs

WOOL

All wool sizes are for felted wool.

¼ yard of red (or red velvet) for top binding on stockings

5" x 8" rectangle of red stripe for heart

7" x 7" square of red for cardinals

9" x 9" square of white for snowman and candy canes

7" x 7" square *each* of 3 greens for holly leaves

3½" x 5" rectangle of green for mistletoe leaves

1" x 1½" rectangle of gold for cardinal beaks

4" x 9" rectangle of brown for branches

1" x 1" square of orange for snowman's carrot nose

4" x 5" rectangle of dark red for snowman's scarf

OTHER MATERIALS

½ yard of 18"-wide lightweight, paper-backed fusible web

13 red buttons, ⅜" to ½" diameter, for holly berries

15 off-white buttons, ¼" to ⅜" diameter, for mistletoe berries

17 off-white buttons, ¼" to ⅝" diameter, for snowflakes

4 lengths, 6" *each*, of black cording for stocking hangers

Thread to match wool colors

Black thread

Template plastic

PEARL COTTON

Colors listed below are for Valdani pearl cotton. See "Resources" on page 111.

Olive Green for holly leaf veins and stems, pine needles on pine sprig, and mistletoe stems

Coffee Roast (dark brown) for pine sprig on snowman

Black for lettering, cardinals' eyes, snowman's mouth, and heart

Aged White Light for snowflakes

Tarnished Gold for cardinals' legs and feet

Old Brick (dark red) for candy cane stripes

CUTTING

From *each of 4* of the dark fat quarters, cut:
5 squares, 6" x 6" (20 total)

From *each* of the 2 remaining dark fat quarters, cut:
6 squares, 6" x 6" (12 total)

From the cream linen, cut:
1 strip, 5" x 40½"

From the red velvet or wool, cut:
4 strips, 2¼" x 13½"

THE STOCKINGS WERE HUNG

MAKING THE STOCKINGS

1. Draw a diagonal line from corner to corner on the wrong side of a dark 6" square. Layer a marked square right sides together with a different dark square. Sew ¼" from each side of the marked line. Cut the squares apart on the drawn line. Press the seam allowances open to reduce bulk. Trim the half-square-triangle unit to measure 5½" x 5½". In the same way, randomly join the dark squares to make a total of 32 half-square-triangle units.

 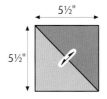

Make 32.

2. Randomly sew units together to make a 40" x 20" pieced rectangle. Press the seam allowances open to reduce bulk. Sew the cream strip to the top of the rectangle as shown. Press the seam allowances open.

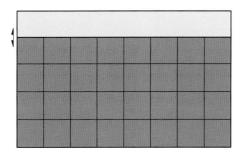

3. Join the top, middle, and bottom sections of the stocking patterns on pages 99–101 along the dashed lines to make a whole stocking pattern. Trace the stocking pattern onto template plastic, being sure to include the straight line on the top section. Cut out the stocking template directly on the line.

4. Align the solid line on the stocking template with the bottom edge of the cream strip and trace around the template to make four stocking fronts. Zigzag stitch around the edges of each stocking to prevent the seams from opening and the fabrics from raveling during the appliqué process.

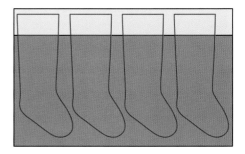

5. Use the stocking template to cut out four reversed stocking backs from the dark-gray flannel. Using the stocking template and the red-print flannel, cut out four stockings and four reversed stockings for the lining.

6. Using a light box and the patterns on page 98, trace the lettering onto the cream part of the stockings, placing the bottom of the lettering ⅝" above the seamline between the cream strip and the patchwork. Using black pearl cotton, outline stitch the lettering. Notice that part of the lettering is two rows of stitches and other parts are only one row of stitching.

Tracing the Lettering

If you don't have a light box, you can tape the design to a window or use a glass-topped table with a lamp underneath.

ADDING THE APPLIQUÉS

Refer to "Working with Wool" on page 107 for detailed information. See "Decorative Stitches" on page 110 as needed.

1. Cut the brown wool into five ⅜" x 9" strips for the branches on the Noël and Peace stockings.

2. Using the patterns on pages 102 and 103, trace each appliqué shape the number of times indicated on the pattern onto the paper side of the fusible web. Cut out each shape

about ⅛" outside the drawn lines. See "Trace to Fit" on page 107.

3. Following the manufacturer's instructions, fuse each shape, glue side down, onto the designated wool color. (Use a variety of different greens for the holly leaves.) Cut out each shape exactly on the drawn line.

4. Using the appliqué pleacement guides below, arrange the appliqué pieces on the background. Pin the branches in place, curving them as shown. Note that you'll need to tuck some pieces under another piece, such as the arm of the snowman under the body. Fuse the appliqué pieces to each stocking's background.

5. Using thread that matches the wool appliqués, whipstitch the pieces in place.

6. Use black pearl cotton to make French knots for the cardinals' eyes and the snowman's mouth. Using black pearl cotton, sew a running stitch around the heart, about ¼" from the edge of the heart.

7. Using brown pearl cotton, outline stitch the pine sprig on the scarf of the snowman.

8. Using gold pearl cotton, embroider two rows of outline stitching for the birds' legs and one row of outline stitching for the birds' feet.

9. Use green pearl cotton and an outline stitch for the veins and stems on the holly leaves, the pine needles on the pine sprig, and the stems of the mistletoe.

10. Use red pearl cotton and two rows of outline stitching for the stripes on the candy canes.

11. Referring to the photos on pages 93 and 95 as a guide, use white pearl cotton and straight stitches to make the small snowflakes on the cardinal stocking. Use the white pearl cotton to sew the snowflake buttons onto the snowman stocking and to stitch the snowflakes that radiate out from the buttons (see the photos on page 98). For the snowflakes, make French knots, straight stitches, lazy daisy stitches, and so on to create your own unique snowflakes.

12. Use black thread to attach the red holly-berry buttons and the off-white mistletoe buttons.

FINISHING

1. Layer an appliquéd stocking front and dark-gray back, right sides together. Using a ¼" seam allowance, sew down one side, around the toe, and up the other side, leaving the top open. Clip the curves and turn the stocking right side out. Press. Make four.

Appliqué placement guides

2. To make the lining, layer one and one reversed red-with-black stockings right sides together. Using a ¼" seam allowance, sew down one side, around the toe, and up the other side, leaving the top open. Clip the curves. *Do not* turn the stocking right side out. Make four.

3. Insert the stocking lining into the stocking so that wrong sides are together and seams are aligned.

4. For the top binding, sew the short ends of one red velvet or wool strip together to make a circle. Place the binding around the top of the stocking, right sides together, so that the raw edges of the stocking, the lining, and the binding are all even. The seam of the binding should be aligned with the seam on the heel side of the stocking. Using a generous ⅜" seam allowance, sew around the top of the stocking. Fold the binding up and over the top of the stocking. Turn the raw edges under and hand sew the binding in place.

5. Fold the black cording in half and tie the ends together as shown to make a hanging loop. Sew the hanging loop in place just inside the top of the stocking where the binding meets the lining along the back seam of the stocking.

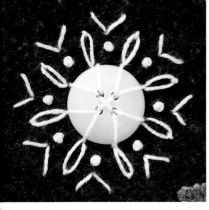

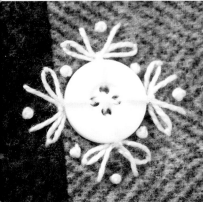

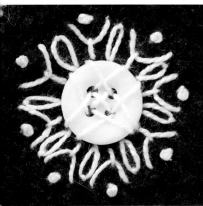

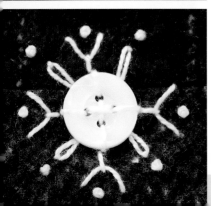

Joy

Love

Peace

Noël

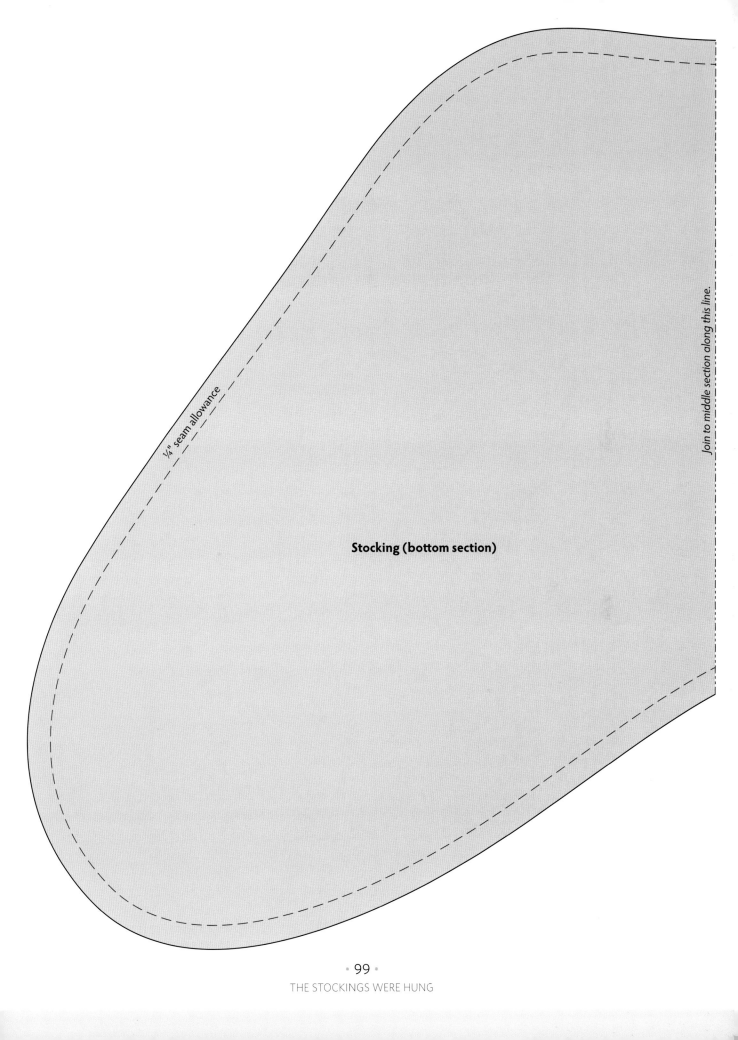

¼" seam allowance

Join to middle section along this line.

Stocking (bottom section)

¼" seam allowance

Stocking (top section)
Cut 4 from patchwork.
Cut 4 reversed from dark-gray herringbone.
Cut 4 and 4 reversed from red-with-black dots.

Align with bottom edge of cream strip.

Join to middle section along this line.

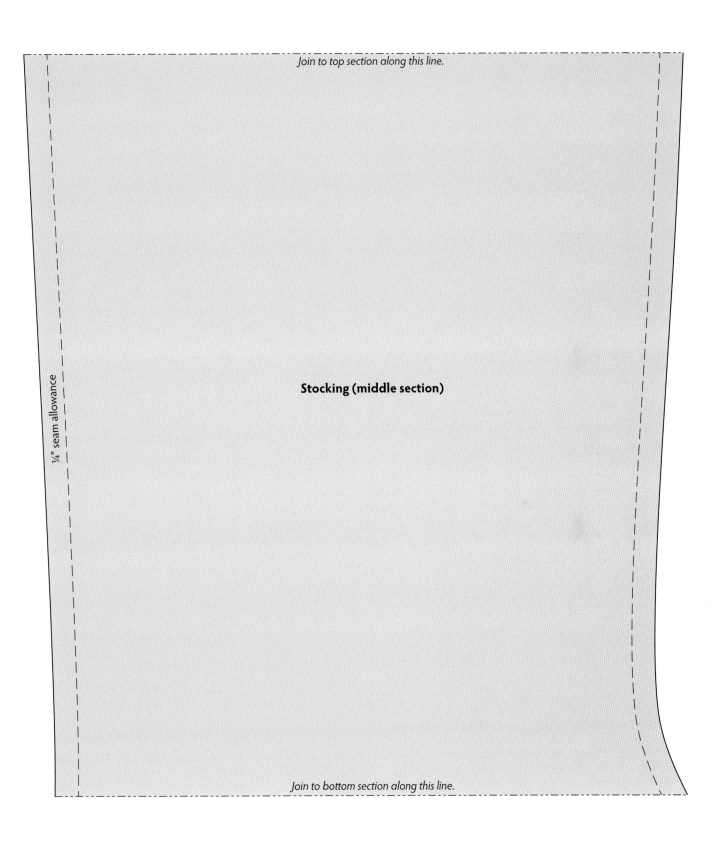

Join to top section along this line.

Stocking (middle section)

¼" seam allowance

Join to bottom section along this line.

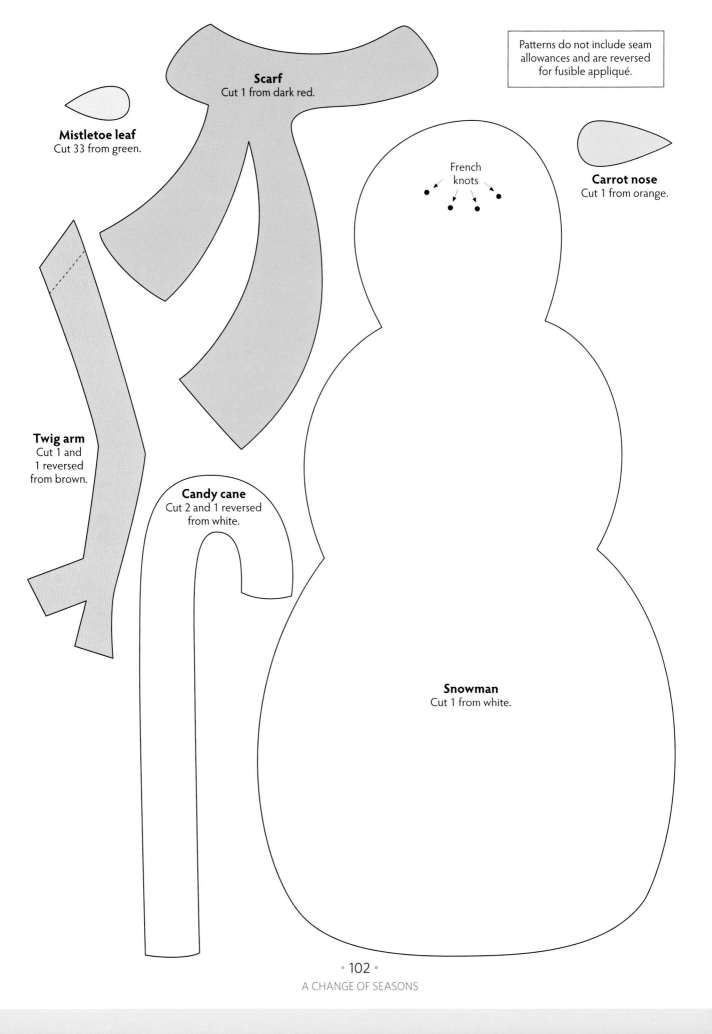

Mistletoe leaf
Cut 33 from green.

Scarf
Cut 1 from dark red.

Patterns do not include seam
allowances and are reversed
for fusible appliqué.

French
knots

Carrot nose
Cut 1 from orange.

Twig arm
Cut 1 and
1 reversed
from brown.

Candy cane
Cut 2 and 1 reversed
from white.

Snowman
Cut 1 from white.

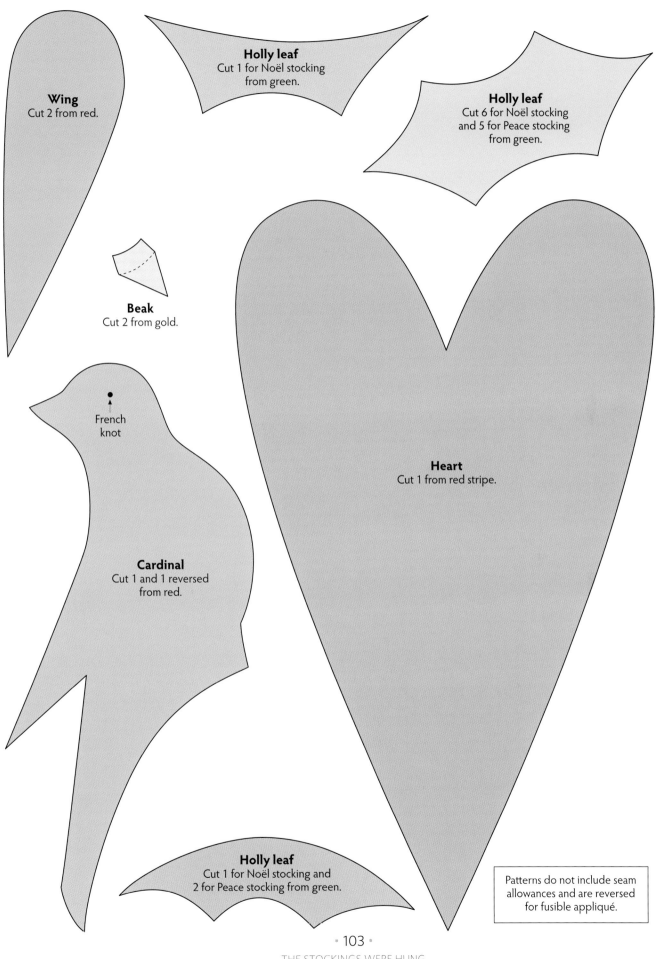

Wing
Cut 2 from red.

Holly leaf
Cut 1 for Noël stocking
from green.

Holly leaf
Cut 6 for Noël stocking
and 5 for Peace stocking
from green.

Beak
Cut 2 from gold.

French
knot

Heart
Cut 1 from red stripe.

Cardinal
Cut 1 and 1 reversed
from red.

Holly leaf
Cut 1 for Noël stocking and
2 for Peace stocking from green.

Patterns do not include seam
allowances and are reversed
for fusible appliqué.

Frosty

designed and made by BONNIE SULLIVAN

*Frosty—wearing a wool scarf against the winter chill—
is here to oversee the holiday festivities.*

FINISHED SIZE: 5" x 9"

WOOL

All wool sizes are for felted wool.

10" x 12½" rectangle of white for snowman
1¼" x 12" strip of red plaid for scarf
1" x 1" square of orange for carrot nose

MUSLIN AND OTHER SUPPLIES

3" x 5" rectangle of muslin for backing
Orange thread
Polyester fiberfill for stuffing
½ cup of small plastic crafting beads, sand, or rice
     for weighting the bottom of the snowman
Small sprig or twig for embellishment
Freezer paper

PEARL COTTON

*Color listed below is for Valdani pearl cotton.
See "Resources" on page 111.*

Black for snowman's mouth and eyes

ASSEMBLING THE SNOWMAN

1. Using the patterns on page 106 and the method
    described on page 108, trace each appliqué
    shape the number of times indicated on the
    pattern onto the unwaxed side of freezer paper.

2. Press the shiny side of each shape onto the right
    side of the designated wool color. Cut out each
    shape exactly on the drawn lines.

3. Place the muslin rectangle on the wrong
    side of the snowman front underneath the
    arm definition lines. Machine stitch the arm
    definition lines. Put a little stuffing in the
    channel between the snowman front and the
    muslin to give the arms a little more definition.
    Trim the excess muslin even with the edges of
    the snowman body.

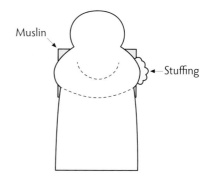

4. With right sides together, sew the snowman's
    front and back together using a ¼" seam
    allowance. Leave the bottom open. Pin and sew
    the base of the snowman to the bottom opening.

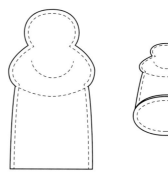

5. Cut a 2" vertical slit in the back of the snowman's body. Turn the snowman right side out through the slit. Pour the small plastic crafting beads, sand, or rice through the slit and shake them down to the bottom of the snowman. Stuff the rest of the snowman with fiberfill and carefully hand sew the slit closed. If you don't like the way the sewn slit looks, appliqué a small heart over the slit or a little pocket that you could tuck a note into.

Cut slit.

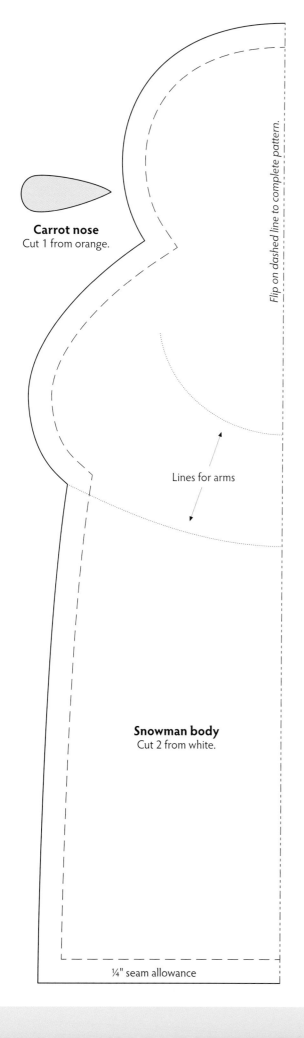

Carrot nose
Cut 1 from orange.

Flip on dashed line to complete pattern.

Lines for arms

Snowman body
Cut 2 from white.

¼" seam allowance

6. Using orange thread, whipstitch the carrot nose in place, hiding the knots in the neck area of the snowman since it will be covered with the scarf.

7. Use two strands of black pearl cotton to make French knots for the mouth and eyes of the snowman. Again hide the knots in the neck area.

8. Remove some of the short threads across the end of the scarf to make a little fringe. Tie the scarf around the snowman's neck.

9. Tack a little sprig or twig in the curve of the snowman's arm.

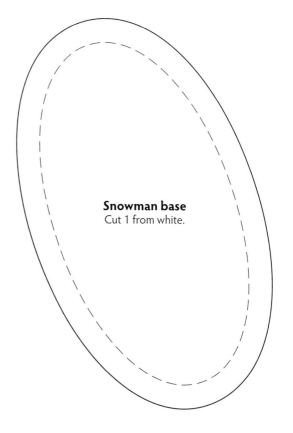

Snowman base
Cut 1 from white.

Bonnie's Techniques

In this section, you'll find some of the basic information you'll need to make the projects in this book. If you're new to sewing and quilting, you can find additional helpful information for free at ShopMartingale.com/HowtoQuilt, where you can download illustrated how-to guides on everything from rotary cutting to binding a quilt.

WORKING WITH WOOL

My knowledge of working with wool has come in bits and pieces over the years. What you'll find here are the methods that work well for me.

Finding and Felting Wool

When I started working with wool, I searched through secondhand stores for 100% wool clothing that I could cut apart and felt. I felt wool by washing it in hot water, rinsing the wool in cold water, and then drying it in a hot dryer. If I want to felt the wool a little more, I repeat the process. Stores that carry fabric for clothing are also good places to find wool, and I felt wool yardage using the same technique. Once I began vending at the International Quilt Market (a wholesale trade show), I found fabulous hand-dyed wools and fell in love with wool even

more. Hand-dyed wool offers a rich, subtle color variation—and as a bonus, it's already been felted. You'll find some of the amazing hand-dyed wool suppliers I use in "Resources" on page 111.

Cutting Out the Appliqués

One of the things I like most about wool appliqué is that you don't have to turn under the edges! Generally, wool doesn't have a right and wrong side. However, you may find that you prefer one side over the other. The side you prefer can be the right side. Following are two different methods I use for cutting out wool appliqué pieces.

Trace to Fit

When I need more than one appliqué shape from one piece of wool, I cut a piece of freezer paper (or fusible web) the same size as the wool piece. I trace all the required appliqué shapes onto the piece of freezer paper (or fusible web), making sure to arrange the shapes so they all fit. Then I press the freezer paper onto the wool and cut out the shapes.

FREEZER PAPER

The first method I ever used, and still use quite often, is the freezer-paper method. An added bonus to using freezer paper is that you can reuse the freezer-paper shapes. So, if a pattern tells you to cut five leaves, you can use the same freezer-paper template for each leaf.

1. Trace the shapes onto the unwaxed side of the freezer paper.

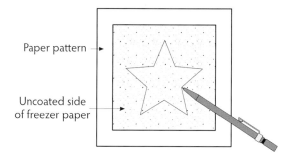

2. Roughly cut out each drawn shape.

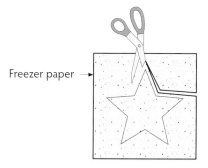

3. Iron the shiny side of the freezer paper onto the *right* side of the wool. Cut out the shapes on the drawn line.

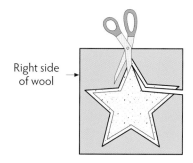

FUSIBLE WEB

The other method I use is fusible appliqué. I've tried a few different fusible webs, but my favorite is Shades' SoftFuse. SoftFuse is very lightweight, pliable, easy to sew through, and it doesn't gum up my needle. When using the fusible method, the pattern pieces need to be traced in reverse. The patterns in this book have already been reversed for you, so they're ready to be traced.

1. Trace the shapes onto the paper side of the fusible web. Roughly cut around each shape.

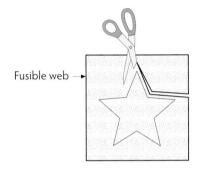

Fusible web →

2. Iron the glue side of the fusible web to the *wrong* side of the wool, following the manufacturer's directions. Cut out the shapes on the drawn line and remove the paper backing.

Wrong side of wool

Paper side of fusible web

3. Press the pieces in place on the right side of the background fabric using plenty of heat to penetrate the wool. Once the pieces are fused in place, turn the pieces over and press them from the wrong side of the background to give the glue the best chance at fusing the layers together.

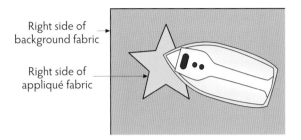

Right side of background fabric →

Right side of appliqué fabric →

Stitching the Pieces

I prefer to stitch the appliqué pieces to the background with a whipstitch. A buttonhole or blanket stitch may be more traditional, but I like the way the stitches seem to disappear when I whipstitch them in place.

The thread I use for whipstitching can be anything from regular sewing thread, to quilting thread, to a single strand of embroidery floss. I'm not particular about what kind of thread I use, but I do match the color to the wool. When whipstitching, I make my stitches about ⅛" apart, a generous ⅛" in length, and perpendicular to the edge of the appliqué piece.

Use matching thread to whipstitch the appliqués in place, keeping the stitches perpendicular to the edge of the appliqué piece.

DECORATIVE STITCHES

All the decorative stitching was done using either size 8 or size 12 pearl cotton. I find that both sizes work equally well. Below are the different decorative stitches used for the projects in this book.

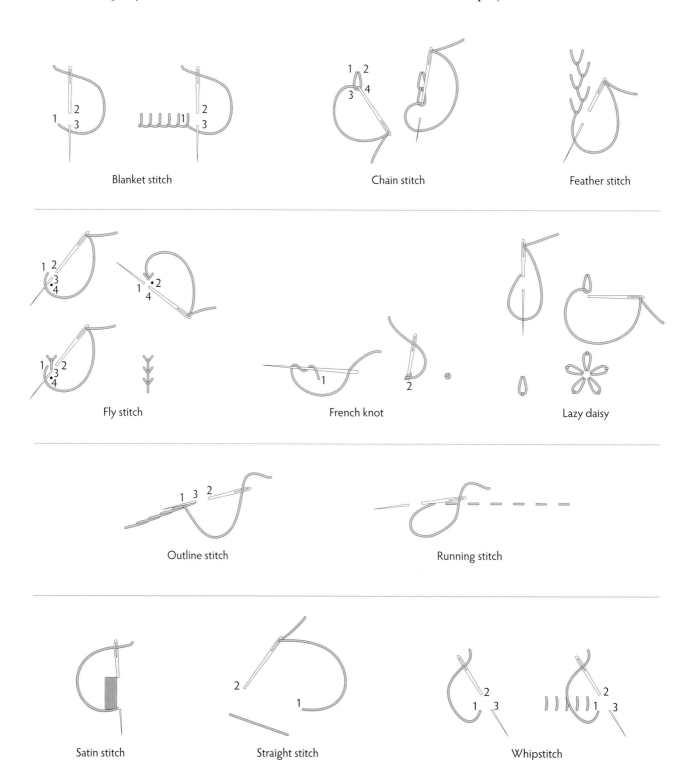

Blanket stitch

Chain stitch

Feather stitch

Fly stitch

French knot

Lazy daisy

Outline stitch

Running stitch

Satin stitch

Straight stitch

Whipstitch

FRAMING A PROJECT

There are four framed projects in this book. The background fabric for each project is oversized, which leaves plenty of extra fabric all the way around your finished piece. Cut a 16" x 20" piece of foam-core board. Center the foam-core board on the wrong side of the appliquéd background using the basting stitches or marked lines as a guide. Wrap the background fabric around the foam-core board and tape it in place, pulling the fabric so it's taut to eliminate wrinkles or sagging on the front. Be careful to not pull the fabric too tight or it will distort. Insert the stitched piece into the frame and secure it with the clips that came with the frame.

Readymade Frames

All of the framed projects in this book are the same size—chosen specifically for a frame with a 16" x 20" opening. This frame size is readily available in a wide variety of styles so you can choose from black, white, barn wood, or everything in between.

Resources

Below is a list of some suppliers of the fabulous goods I used in this book! If you can't find what you need at your local shop, try these websites.

WOOL

Blackberry Primitives
www.BlackberryPrimitives.com

Mary Flanagan Woolens
www.MFWoolens.com

PEARL COTTON

Valdani
www.Valdani.com
Valdani has assembled a thread pack of the pearl cottons I used in this book, called A Change of Seasons by Bonnie Sullivan of All Through the Night. The colors I used are: P2 (Olive Green), H202 (Withered Green), P5 (Tarnished Gold), P6 (Rusted Orange), P1 (Old Brick), O513 (Coffee Roast), O178 (Tea-Dyed Stone), P4 (Aged White Light), P11 (Aged Black), 1 (Black), and 3 (White).

FLANNEL

Maywood Studio
www.MaywoodStudio.com
All the flannel fabrics used in this book are from Maywood's Woolies line.

For as long as I can remember, I've always loved textiles—I still have remnants of my childhood blanket. My neighbor taught me how to embroider when I was seven. My mother taught 4-H sewing, and I spent many childhood hours making troll and Barbie doll clothes. I remember being fascinated by the quilts my grandmother and mother pieced and hand quilted. There is just something comforting about working with fabrics and wools, and the textures and colors have captivated me from a very young age. I never thought I'd be designing and creating for a living, but I'm thankful every day for the opportunity.

I was introduced to working with wool in 2000 and was immediately hooked. After designing several penny-rug patterns, I thought I would try my luck at the International Quilt Market and attended my first show as a vendor in May of 2002. My business quickly grew and in 2003, I began designing fabric for Maywood Studio. Because I love working with wool, I designed a line of flannels called Woolies to look like wool. The Woolies line has gone through many transformations over the years, adding new colors and textures. I love combining the Woolies flannels with wool, and all four of the quilts in this book are made with a combination of the two. Please visit my website at AllThroughtheNight.net.